CEMETERIES:
Alive with Learning

BARBARA KISSLING

National Middle School Association
Westerville, Ohio

April Tibbles, Director of Publications

John Lounsbury, Editor, Professional Publications

Carla Weiland, Publications Editor

Ann Draghi, Graphic Designer

Dawn Williams, Publications Manager

Marcia Meade-Hurst, Senior Publications Representative

Derek Neal, Publications & Membership Marketing Manager

Library of Congress Cataloging-in-Publication Data

Kissling, Barbara.
    Cemeteries : alive with learning / Barbara Kissling.
        p. cm.
    Includes bibliographical references.
    ISBN 978-1-56090-238-6
    1. School field trips. 2. Cemeteries--Study and teaching (Middle school). 3. Science--Study and teaching (Middle school). 4. History--Study and teaching (Middle school) 5. Middle school education--Activity programs. I. Title.
    LB1047.K55 2010
    373.13'84--dc22
                                    2010010411

National Middle School Association
4151 Executive Parkway, Suite 300
Westerville, Ohio 43081
1-800-528-NMSA f: 614-895-4750
www.nmsa.org

Acknowledgements

The idea for a cemetery project goes back many years to a conference session I attended on cemetery activities. Then, years later, a grant opportunity brought to life this long dormant idea and made it a reality. The mysterious attraction of a cemetery became an underlying factor in the creation and conduct of an incredible educational adventure that involved the academic subjects and service learning. Many realistic and meaningful activities evolved from the ideas of students and adults.

I owe so many people a great deal, ones who were directly involved in the project and ones who helped in producing this book. Accolades go to my patient husband who was always there to help me; my son, Mark, and his wife, Erica, for their encouragement; Cindy Scarlett and Dr. Grayson Wheatley for their assistance with planning and writing the grant; Marilyn Hala from the Toyota TIME Grant program who was always very positive; Suzanne Sullivan, my team teacher, who bravely joined me on this adventure; Barbara Hoevel, my principal, for her support; Elaine Davis, a research historian, who greatly enriched this project with her expertise; and to John Lounsbury and Carla Weiland, National Middle School Association editors, for their belief in my manuscript and their conscientious work in editing it.

And last, and most important, I thank the students and their parents who enthusiastically participated in the cemetery activities. Giving my students a rich and active learning experience was my motivation for creating this project, and they responded as only young adolescents can.

Barbara Kissling

Contents

CHAPTER

"Study a Cemetery???"

A cemetery is a great laboratory for learning. It may be a place of mystery and even scary to some, but it is also an environment overflowing with learning opportunities. Teachers have often used cemeteries to study local history with their students, but seldom have the educational riches of cemeteries been tapped sufficiently. With a cemetery-based study, all teachers can enrich their teaching. Interdisciplinary teams find that the cemetery is the perfect locale for carrying out an integrated learning experience. The varied and engaging activities possible in a cemetery project make learning experiences real and meaningful. Such projects will fulfill the recommendation that an effective middle level curriculum be "challenging, exploratory, integrative, and relevant" (National Middle School Association, 2010, p.17).

In recent years formal education has become overly focused on standardized testing and teaching to the test at the expense of creative projects. Faithfully covering a test-oriented curriculum has forced teachers to forego many hands-on activities that engage students and connect subject areas. A cemetery project, however, can bring imaginative activities back into the curriculum as students master skills that will meet state requirements and effectively prepare for standardized tests.

This book describes the development and implementation of a successful long-term cemetery project and provides information, ideas, and suggestions that will help you envision and plan your own cemetery-based study. As you read this story, you will intuitively sense comparable things you or your team could do. Drawing on the activities and resources included here, you can tailor a project that fits your particular situation and would advance the learning goals you have in a new and more meaningful way.

The skeleton of a cemetery project can be established and shaped with the inquiry approach involving one or more overarching questions and related sub-questions to tie the activities together. As the project develops, students' curiosity and interests always generate new directions for inquiry that broaden the scope of study even further. I found that between my own ideas and those of my students and their parents, we had many questions and subsequent activities to consider—more than we had time to do.

Adaptability of cemetery projects

Cemetery-based activities can be used with any age group, class, or teaming situation. I was part of Team Explore, a two person team, and I had prime responsibility for math and science while my teaching partner was the language arts and social studies specialist. We worked on some cemetery activities in our individual classes, while other activities were done in large group sessions. A cemetery project can work in almost any organizational configuration from a single subject class to a whole team project that draws on many subjects in an integrated, thematic unit.

A project can range from a one-day, intensive field trip with pre- and post-visit classroom work, to being the focus of learning for a whole semester or a year or more. Parents, community members, and local or state organizations are likely to become involved and service learning opportunities are often present.

Activity Examples

The following are examples of the diverse kinds of activities that can be developed in a cemetery-based project.

- After reading tombstone inscriptions, students create fictional epitaphs or obituaries for themselves, other persons they know, or for a person buried there whose life they have researched.

- Researching the lives of people buried in a cemetery through old newspapers or census records reveals much about a community's history and culture.

- The analysis of tombstones for rock composition and weathering offers a science lesson more realistic than looking at rock samples in a classroom.

- Tombstone inscriptions provide a wealth of data for a study of statistics as well as other math topics including fractions, decimals, and percents.

- Using technology such as a GPS assists students in creating a cemetery map, even a topographic one.

- The process of applying for a historical marker is the basis for a significant service learning experience.

What can be accomplished with a cemetery project will depend on many factors including access to a cemetery, time available to work in it, existing curriculum expectations, the support of the administration and others, and your imagination. But this much is certain: a cemetery-based study will be a highly effective way to meet already established goals and prepare students for

A cemetery is a place to study the present as much as the past.

whatever standardized tests lie ahead. It is not a detour but a better road on which to travel in quest of academic achievement.

There are a number of educational materials on cemeteries available on the Internet. The website created by Linda Prather is filled with information, suggestions, and related resources that are just one click away (www.angelfire.com/ky2/cemetery). This Kentucky teacher has been doing cemetery studies for years—"They beg to go back"—and has been recognized for her work. The story of the Annual Evergreen Cemetery Discovery Walk can be viewed at http://www.uhigh.ilstu.edu/laptops/promisingpractices/englishcollaboration.pdf and is one of a number of such cemetery projects now conducted in schools. The Vermont Old Cemetery Association compiled a resource packet of cemetery information and random activities collected by teachers in that area entitled "Stones & Bones" (Vermont Old Cemetery Association, 1996, http://www.sover.net/~hwdbry/voca/). Materials in the packet range from an article on burial customs and cemeteries in American history to "grave" humor. Additional sources for related materials will be cited throughout the various chapters.

Cemeteries: Alive with Learning evolved from the limited use of a nearby cemetery for science activities to a project that integrated multiple subject areas. The tremendous success of the project is the impetus for this book. I hope it will inspire teachers and provide them both with the encouragement and the specific ideas they need to create meaningful learning experiences for their students in a place-based educational adventure.

How it all began

It was a dreary November day. School was over for the day, and I was reading the mail that I had just picked up in the office. One piece was a brochure advertising the Toyota TIME Grant program. What really caught my eye was a free trip to Las Vegas, the location of the National Council of Teachers of Mathematics annual conference! What did I need to do to get a trip to Las Vegas? I went back to the beginning of the brochure to find out.

The brochure indicated that to encourage innovative school projects, the Toyota TIME program would award two-year grants to teachers with projects that would enhance mathematics education. I immediately thought about the cemetery I had used to conduct science lessons. Every year when I had visited the cemetery, I saw what a huge impression it had on my students. They liked the idea of taking a field trip to such an unusual place. The physical activity and freedom of being in the cemetery working with tombstones to gather data or make rubbings excited them, and they always had questions about the names and data on the tombstones. Their curiosity and emotional reaction were just too powerful to ignore, and I knew I would have to build on them. So when the Toyota grant possibility came along, I was ready to jump in and never look back. I could develop a math-centered cemetery project. Data from tombstones could be used in place of textbook data for statistics and in other areas of math. Such endeavors were possible so proceeding with the application was an easy decision.

The application required a description of the potential impact the project would have on students and how it could be measured. Improvement in test scores alone, while important, did not seem to be enough since many of the students in our team were already at or above grade level in math achievement. I was very concerned, however, about students' attitudes towards math. Many strongly disliked it and saw little use for it in their daily lives. Textbook data seemed artificial and trivial to them. In contrast, data derived from tombstones represented real people. Would this make a difference to students? I decided to promote positive student attitudes in math as one of my grant goals.

The grant guidelines presented some suggestions for developing a quality project such as connecting math with other disciplines and using technology for learning math. Wow! I knew I could do those things, even though I wasn't exactly sure how just yet. I began personal brainstorming, talking to other educators, collecting ideas from conferences I had attended, and reviewing educational resources. I soon came up with a list of activities that represented the four main academic areas and service learning. A lot of details were called for in the proposal, yet I left some wiggle room for change as the project unfolded. I particularly wanted students to have a part in planning what we did.

I submitted the final application on time, but with limited hope of receiving a national grant. A few months later, however, the principal walked into my classroom with a smile on her face and informed me that I had received one of 35 Toyota TIME grants. It included the trip to Las Vegas to attend the National Council of Teachers of Mathematics Conference and a whole lot more.

Engaging in a cemetery project does not require special funding, but the grant provided $9,300 that was well-used. Since my 6th graders were unfamiliar with graphing calculators, I thought they would be interested in learning to use them for graphing tombstone data. Thus, about a third of the money went for calculators, an overhead teacher calculator, and a digital camera—which I threw in at the last minute and used constantly! The rest of the money was for staff development (calculator training, conferences, etc.), substitute teachers, and supplies.

If I had not received the grant, funding for such expenditures might have been available through regular school sources, the parent-teacher group, or the school district's educational foundation. Local historical societies, civic clubs, and community service groups are also good sources for money, particularly if planned projects will improve a public cemetery or other community entity. However, a cemetery-based learning experience does not require any special funding.

I appreciated the grant because it pushed me to do a project that I might not have done otherwise, and, in the process, I discovered a creative side of me that I never knew existed. It led me to think more about student attitudes and making math and science more relevant for students beyond what I was already attempting. The project also allowed me to move into integrated learning involving a variety of other subject areas. The incorporation of technology made it possible for me to learn how to use new equipment and instructional strategies. I grew personally and professionally and believe strongly that a cemetery-based project would be more than worth doing for any teacher or team. It can fit into the curriculum of any subject or better yet integrate multiple areas and make learning come alive for students while meeting national standards. There are a host of positive reasons for incorporating a cemetery project into a curriculum; many have already been identified, while others will be highlighted in the pages to follow.

Now, we begin our examination of a cemetery-based study by considering its planning and preparation.

CHAPTER

Planning and Preparation

Planning for a cemetery-based study is not a task that can be done quickly. There are many things to be considered beyond the usual planning for instruction—and they do require some extra time and effort. But, as will become evident from the engagement and enthusiasm of the students, such special work will prove to be a sound investment for a professional teacher. Resources like this book and websites on the Internet provide assistance with designing a cemetery study and activities for it, but ultimately the project has to be planned by those who will carry it out in each particular situation.

Selecting a cemetery

One of the first decisions to be made is selecting a cemetery. This decision may be determined partly by the goals you have in mind, but at the same time your goals may be determined by the nature of the cemetery selected. There are so many factors to be considered including location, accessibility, number of visits needed, the length of time available to make visits, and possible leads to broaden the study, not to mention specific curriculum concerns. A project that is focused primarily on one subject may require only a single visit while a project that draws on several subjects may require additional visits spread over time. Field trip options might be one day, two days with one early in the school year and the other much later, several days in a row, or any variation that fits your situation and permits you to accomplish your goals. The first year you may want to limit the initial scope of your project, but once into it, you will find it has a way of growing.

Unless you are lucky as I was and have a cemetery in walking distance, visiting a cemetery involves transportation, which can be costly. Funds have to be secured from an already budgeted field trip fund, the parent-teacher organization, or other source, and the cost may determine the number of cemetery visits you make. For long visits, restroom availability is an issue that has to be addressed.

Safety is always a matter of concern. Many cemeteries are huge and students could easily wander off. Only a portion of the cemetery might be used for the project, and students would have to be aware of boundary lines. Parent chaperones can be very helpful with "policing" these lines. If the tombstones are in poor condition and might topple over or the grounds are overgrown or very uneven, such a location would not be a safe environment for students.

The quality of tombstones and the inscription and artwork on them might be a factor in choosing a cemetery. Since weathering often destroys the lettering, a good number of legible tombstones must be available. If the tombstones have epitaphs beyond the basic facts of a person's name, birth and death date, and age at death, such additional information is likely to be helpful for lessons in language arts and social studies. For art related activities, very old tombstones reflecting early American folk art by their shape, carving, and symbolism provide a rich source of material to study. The composition of a variety of tombstones provides a genuine geology lesson in rock types and which rocks survive weathering the best. Many newly established cemeteries do not accept upright tombstones and would lack some of the learning opportunities described above, but provide other opportunities.

Another consideration in selecting a cemetery is the people who are buried there. Does the cemetery contain the graves of community founders or notable people in community history who might warrant being studied in some detail? Would a church cemetery be desirable to trace the history of families within a congregation? In a city owned or public cemetery, do people seem to be related and buried in family plots or are there mostly individual graves? Do any of the graves have a special designation for veterans? A military cemetery would certainly be interesting as it would reflect time spans that covered several wars or conflicts. And for some studies, two different cemeteries might be used.

My own choice for a cemetery was easy because it is located a 20-minute walk from school, and our team could go there and back during our instructional block of time and still have forty-five minutes for activities on site. Some years our block of time was too short for the activities planned, and we asked for permission to keep students for an additional period. Another cemetery that was located a few miles away had interesting tombstones of the "founding families" of the community, but it was larger and very hilly with overgrown shrubbery. Actually, I was pleased with our small cemetery with plain tombstones because it was non-threatening to 6th graders and had been part of the county poor farm. This history would provide a good opportunity for students in our comfortable suburban community to learn about a poor farm and identify with people who had much less. But any cemetery, every cemetery, is alive with learning opportunities and can support meaningful activities. A cemetery study is not a matter of introducing new material to be covered in an already overcrowded curriculum so much as it is a matter of providing an approach and a strategy for more effectively meeting already stated goals and responsibilities.

After a cemetery is selected, securing permission to take students there to complete various activities is necessary. When I began the project, I called several county offices and ended up communicating with a gentleman in charge of the county-owned apartments near the cemetery. He was delighted with our interest in the cemetery and was very helpful as we worked through various phases of the project.

Determining major goals

With a cemetery selected, the next step is firming up the goals you want to accomplish. The Toyota grant requirements were critical in shaping my initial goals. Since the grant was math-based, my primary goals were to promote positive student attitudes and performance in math. These were realistic and achievable goals because cemetery-based studies involve many factors or conditions that positively impact motivation and learning. They:

- Capture student interest with a unique learning environment.
- Provide hands-on activities for all ability levels.
- Encourage critical thinking.
- Connect subjects and integrate learning experiences.
- Relate to the community and its history.
- Permit meaningful learning apart from textbooks and the classroom.
- Utilize cooperative group work.
- Involve technology or digital tools such as various computer programs, digital cameras, and web pages.
- Provide service learning opportunities.

Given these conditions, I knew our project would be successful, as would any project that has the realism a cemetery provides.

After deciding on a few specific goals, I formulated plans for achieving them. I focused first on the tombstone data and incorporated it into the statistics unit in math. I used activities planned during the summer to start the school year and then developed additional activities throughout the year as the project progressed. A highlight event near the end of the study is important to develop. In my case, the first year's special activity was acquiring a historical marker, and the second year's was preparing and publishing a booklet about the cemetery. At the end of each year we also shared our activities and findings in an evening presentation for parents and others. Students were proud of their accomplishments and insisted that these events be relatively gala affairs.

Improving student attitudes and achievement in math turned out to be simply my starting goals. As the project developed, other goals and activities evolved from what we were doing. Questions from our study of tombstone data led to historical research. Then, with the encouragement of students, we became committed to learning more about the history of the poor farm. We were using the inquiry method to make sense of things that happened in the past that differed from the present and our perception of the past. The more we studied the cemetery, the more our goals and subsequent activities snowballed.

I had a personal goal to get students to care about other people, and in this case, people they never knew and who were no longer alive. The people whose tombstones we were studying had been residents of a poor farm and may have been homeless, chronically ill, or mentally disabled. They were buried in the poor farm cemetery because when they died, no one claimed their bodies for burial. As we studied the history of the poor farm and found out more about its residents, many students were touched by what we discovered and wanted to do something to improve the cemetery. Planting flowers was an early improvement effort, while obtaining and appropriately displaying an official historical marker was a very time consuming but most worthwhile service learning experience.

At first, conducting a project over the course of a school year and achieving all my goals seemed overwhelming. To ease my anxiety in planning, I found it helpful to divide the project into manageable parts rather than think of it always as a whole. I prepared a timeline and focused on the units and activities that needed to be addressed first. This planning included glancing ahead to see if an upcoming activity or event required advance work or the creation of some worksheet. From year to year I would solicit student input in picking and choosing what activities worked best within such constraints as class time available and my teaching schedule. For example, in the second year of the project, the school's advisory program was unfortunately eliminated and we lost that time for large group sessions. Most important, the activities we did during school time had to mesh with the district's curriculum guidelines.

Preparation for the visit

The amount and nature of preparation needed for a cemetery project obviously depends on the various goals and activities you plan. For the first year, a significant amount of my preparation for the project occurred before the school year began. Although I usually planned new lessons or units and attended classes during the summer, the project required more. I realized that I needed to consult with a variety of people, learn new technology, and design cemetery related surveys and activities.

Communicating about the project with other people is always important before and throughout the implementation. Sharing information with your principal and seeking his or her support is critical. I had met with my principal during the previous school year when I was applying for the grant. The application required her signature, and this gave me an opportunity to share my ideas and get her endorsement. I also talked with my team teacher, Suzanne, about participating in the project, and during the summer we met and did some preliminary planning. Additionally, prior to the start of school and throughout the year, I communicated often with our school technology coordinator.

Preparation in my case also involved buying and using new equipment. I was surprised how much time it took to figure out which graphing calculator was appropriate for the project and what supplementary materials would be needed. A university math education professor was very helpful with these decisions. Buying an appropriate digital camera was a difficult matter until I contacted a technology teacher from the intermediate school district for a recommendation. Learning how to use the new equipment and computer programs was another challenge, but meeting it was completely worth the time and effort. The grant paid for a week at a college in Pennsylvania during the summer for instruction in using the graphing calculator. I also took free computer classes at the intermediate school district to learn the different programs I would use in the project—Designing a Website, PowerPoint, Excel, Digital Photography, Photoshop, and more.

The first field trip to the cemetery provided an obvious starting point for my planning. This visit was to collect data and make tombstone rubbings. During the summer, I drew two maps of tombstone locations in the cemetery because the tombstones were arranged differently on the left side of the cemetery than the right side. Students would use these maps to find their assigned tombstones and record data from them for our studies in math class. Then, to prepare for tombstone rubbings, I experimented with several different kinds of paper and crayons before concluding that newsprint worked best. Even if the study you are considering is not focused on history or numerical data, doing tombstone rubbings is always an interesting and engaging activity that gets them "into" the cemetery and opens the way for other activities.

Assessing the learning

Assessments for the project depend on the goals and activities you select. In the basic subject areas you would have existing curriculum guidelines and can assess students as you normally do with tests, writing samples, lab reports, group projects, and the like. But obviously these checks are not likely to touch many important goals. Surveys are an appropriate way to gain information before doing some activities, for an informal evaluation after non-graded activities, or on the project as a whole. Verbal and written feedback from students is always important because it helps you to determine if the project activities are meeting stated goals.

The assessment component of my grant required the development of several surveys. When I started thinking about surveying the students before the first cemetery visit, I realized its importance. Students might be uncomfortable going to a cemetery because of a death in their family or for religious or cultural-based reasons. Upon our return from the visit, informal discussion and a written response that was completed as homework gave me an opportunity to assess what students learned and how they felt about being in a cemetery. To evaluate student attitudes on working with cemetery data in math, I had students complete a survey both before and after the statistics unit. In June, a final survey assessed the success of the project as a whole.

There were several other forms of assessment for the grant besides subject area evaluations and surveys. Standardized tests were used in math to check for improvement in scores from the beginning of the school year to the end. Informal assessments included student presentations to the team about special after school activities related to the cemetery project and presentations to other audiences such as the Parent Teacher Organization about the cemetery project as a whole. It was amazing to see some students speak comfortably in front of a large group about our cemetery studies. Last, and certainly not least, were the lively class discussions that ranged from speculation on inconsistent math data, to information found on census forms, to how other cultures or societies deal with death – critical thinking in action. Students freely shared their opinions and asked many questions. The presentations and discussions were not graded, but they certainly served as a way for me to know what the students were learning and how they were processing this knowledge and trying to make sense of it all.

Doing rubbings of tombstones immediately gives students a close and personal identification with these sources of data.

Preparing students and parents

How should the idea of a cemetery-based study be introduced to a team of sixth graders? The idea is still rather unusual so beginning on a positive note is important. I started during the first week of school with a PowerPoint presentation showing photographs of the cemetery and a picture of a graphing calculator. The presentation outlined the main topics we would study and highlighted some of the planned activities. These made evident the clear academic legitimacy of what we would be doing. The presentation took about ten minutes, and then I answered questions. The students—remember they had just entered our school—were surprised with the project, but seemed ready to try something different. By the second year of the project, of course, students had heard about it and looked forward to participating in it.

Good communication with parents is always important, but in this case it is critical. Not only is it important to explain this new and different school project, but also, you must gain parents' support and assistance with it. They are particularly helpful as chaperones when visiting the cemetery and as drivers for after school field trips. To communicate with parents, I first sent them our team newsletter that included a paragraph about the cemetery project. At Open House I used the same PowerPoint presentation that I had shown the students and emphasized how this project would fit in with the current curriculum and provide many new and engaging learning experiences. Throughout the school year, I informed parents about the project in our weekly team newsletter. Many parents listened daily to our Homework Hotline, which was another opportunity to share information on the project's progress and upcoming activities. Parents were always eager to hear about the project and regularly had suggestions for additional activities.

I also used the PowerPoint presentation for various groups early in the year until I had enough pictures with students participating in activities to develop a new one. When we shared our project with groups like the Parent Teacher Organization or the Historical Commission, students assumed the role of narrating the presentation. Before each presentation, students would choose what specifically they wanted to talk about. Eventually, we did not even use the PowerPoint presentation, and students simply showed examples of their work, such as tombstone rubbings and graphs, when they spoke. It was impressive to hear students deliver their talks. Only occasionally did I have to fill in with explanations.

At the beginning of the second school year, I arranged a bulletin board with pictures taken from various activities during the first year. I titled it "What's happening here?" I made no comments about the bulletin board, but waited for students to notice it and start asking questions. It piqued their curiosity and proved to be an excellent way to capture their attention.

Both years, I found very few students and their parents who initially had a difficult time understanding why and how a cemetery would be used for a school project. For most, their only contact with a cemetery was attending a funeral, and it was hard for them to get beyond that experience and visualize the cemetery as a teaching and learning laboratory. Once they had the opportunity to see and understand what we were doing, they realized the value of the project with its wide variety of learning experiences, and they joined right in.

In summary

For a teacher or team, working with a cemetery begins with a commitment to provide a unique project for students. The cemetery is chosen, goals are selected, and a loose framework with activities is established that gives security at the start but is open enough to allow change as the project progresses. The cemetery project can be as simple or detailed as circumstances permit. It can start and stay small with one or two activities or it can increase in size. Additional activities can be added that bring in additional subject areas. A team of teachers can implement an integrated project that occurs for one unit or throughout the school year. It is a bonus to have students help with the project, determining some of the activities, and thus taking ownership of it. Likewise, service learning activities, such as cleaning up the cemetery in some way, can take place.

In Chapter 3, the project actually begins for students with that eagerly awaited visit to the cemetery; the chapter tells about what they did there and concludes with the follow-up activities.

CHAPTER

The Cemetery Visit

Visiting a cemetery for the first time is a significant event for most students. Some may have a bit of apprehension about it, but all are eager to go. To maximize this learning experience teachers must address the three phases that comprise such a trip: planning and preparation before the visit, the actual visit with students involved in selected activities, and after the visit, a debriefing session and follow-up activities.

Preparation before the trip

Planning and preparation begin with checking out the cemetery. In my case, although I had been there many times before, I needed to see it anew, note any hazards, and sketch out maps for the students to use. Drawing maps to show the location of tombstones was necessary because each pair of students would be assigned to four specific tombstones for data collection. Visiting the cemetery after it has been selected as the site inevitably will also give rise to possibilities not previously considered.

Timing of the first visit is a critical part of the planning. An early fall field trip was important for our project because we had to collect the cemetery data before starting the statistics unit in math. I usually began the school year with statistics, but because time was needed to type the data into the computer, I switched statistics with a unit on factors and multiples without disrupting the overall flow of the math curriculum. It was a challenge, however, to take a field trip during the first week or two of school when I was just getting to know students as individuals.

Weather is another factor to consider in setting a time for a visit. Living in a cold climate forced me to settle on early fall and mid-spring visits for the team. I always set a date with an alternate one in case of inclement weather. Going too late in the spring would be a problem if the weather were hot or there were too many hungry female mosquitoes present.

Before taking the first trip to the cemetery, I had students complete a brief "Explore the Past Survey" to see if they had any concerns about going there. In reading their comments, I identified a few that I had to talk to privately. When I answered their questions and gave additional details, they usually felt comfortable and were ready to go on the field trip. In the many years of going to the cemetery, I had only one student who did not want to go and chose to work on an assignment in the library instead. By the next trip to the cemetery, however, he had changed his mind and decided to go with the team.

Preparing for the field trip also involved filling out the appropriate forms with the school office and notifying the faculty with at least a memo in their mailboxes. To inform parents and secure their permission, I sent out a letter describing the cemetery visit with a permission slip to be signed and returned. Even though parents had already given permission on emergency cards filed in the office for regular field trips, I wanted to be sure that parents knew exactly what we were doing. The letter included an invitation for parents to accompany us on the walk to the cemetery or meet us there to assist students in collecting data and doing tombstone rubbings.

A few parents did not give permission initially because they felt it would be disrespectful for students to be in a cemetery. When I called them and explained that our cemetery project was a way in which to honor those buried there and that student behavior on our visit would be carefully monitored, they readily gave permission. I urged these parents to join us and sometimes they did. One of my favorite memories was observing a previously hesitant parent with her child leaning over a grave doing a tombstone rubbing. They were so intent on the rubbing that they were oblivious to the grave beneath them.

Getting ready to go

Proper student behavior in the cemetery was an absolute requirement. On the day I handed out the parent letter, we discussed what might be dubbed "cemetery etiquette" thoroughly. I asked students what they would consider proper behavior in a cemetery. They came up with the following list, which we wrote on poster board:

- no fooling around
- walk, don't run
- use normal voices
- do not sit on the tombstones
- work on the assignment
- leave no trash

On the day of the trip, we reviewed the list. Student behavior, I am glad to report, was never a problem on any of our visits.

After the behavior reminder, I asked students to choose a partner for our cemetery activities, and I handed out the following materials to each pair of students:

- clipboard
- two maps of the cemetery—the left side and the right side
- four tombstone information sheets

I explained how to read the cemetery maps and pointed out that each pair of students would find four tombstones circled on one of their maps. Their assignment was to find those tombstones and copy the information from them onto the tombstone information sheets. Each tombstone had a separate sheet. Once they finished recording the data for the four tombstones and handed in their sheets, they would have time to do tombstone rubbings with newsprint and crayons.

Supplies I took to the cemetery were:

- camera
- bug spray
- cell phone
- band aids
- manila folders, marked 1 to 12, for numbering tombstone rows
- toothbrushes for cleaning tombstone lettering if needed (students can bring from home)
- newsprint and crayons
- trash bag

I always took a camera with me to capture images for later use on bulletin boards, the website, school newsletters, posters, or in a PowerPoint. I also found it helpful to ask a parent or an interested student to take pictures that would free me to concentrate on overseeing the activity and talk to students.

On the day of the cemetery visit, I allotted a two-hour block of time for the field trip. The walk from the school to the cemetery was about twenty minutes, but we stopped along the way at the location of the original poor farm building for a brief history lesson. The current apartment building dated back to 1929 when the poor farm had evolved into a hospital. The Medical Care Facility next door was an outgrowth of the poor farm hospital and now serves the community as a nursing home and rehabilitative center. We would expand on these topics considerably as the project continued throughout the school year.

Activities on site

When we arrived at the cemetery, I laid down the manila folders numbering the tombstone rows. Students then used their maps to find the row with their assigned tombstones. Parents assisted students who had difficulty finding the location of their tombstones. Toothbrushes were available to clean off the indented lettering if it was difficult to read due to dirt or moss. On some tombstones the lettering was illegible due to weathering. Tombstones that were completely illegible were recorded as such because their existence would still be important for the statistics study.

Students copied inscriptions on the tombstone information sheet (Figure 3.1), which I had prepared. This form called for recording the tombstone's location by row and number, the person's name, date of birth, date of death, age at death, and an indication of the tombstone's condition. Parents were helpful in figuring out unusual names and hard-to-read inscriptions. I told students to do the best they could and guess where necessary. In this cemetery the graves were placed chronologically by year of death, which helped determining the year in cases where the inscription was not clear. At times, students had to record "cannot read." Because this was a poor farm cemetery, tombstones were very plain and lacked information and decoration found in many cemeteries. Name, date of death, and age at death were the only details usually available on these tombstones.

After recording tombstone data on worksheets, students made tombstone rubbings. Some trial and error usually took place as students figured out how to get a good impression. It seemed to work best when one student held the newsprint on the tombstone while another one used a crayon to rub over the lettering. Students often peeled the paper off the crayon and used the side of it to rub rather than the tip. Sometimes rubbings were difficult to read close up, but were much more legible if viewed from a distance. Students learned that badly weathered tombstones produced poor rubbings. It is important to note

Figure 3.1 Tombstone Information Sheet

Cemetery location: row number_____

Tombstone information

_____

_____

_____

_____

_____

_____

Using the above information, fill in the blanks below. Write NA (not available) if a blank cannot be filled in.

1. First name of person _____

2. Middle name of person _____

3. Last name of person _____

4. Date of birth _____

5. Date of death_____

6. Age at death _____

Tombstone condition – circle the appropriate answer

Unsteady tombstone (moves)	Yes	No
Tombstone damaged	Yes	No
Letters hard to read	Yes	No

that using a toothbrush to clean the letters or even doing a rubbing may not be allowed in some cemeteries—something to check on ahead of time.

Students had time to walk around and explore the cemetery after they had completed their assignments. They looked at different tombstones and had a variety of observations to share. The many graves of babies caught their attention. They were curious about why there were so many, which led to some discussion of infant mortality in times past. Students questioned some of the unusual names on the tombstones, and some noticed the varying ages at which people died. One girl commented to me that a man had died on her birth date. The comments students made to one another and to me were indications that the curiosity that characterizes young adolescents was being fed and that an emotional attachment to the cemetery was beginning to develop.

After forty-five minutes, students had completed their data collection, finished several rubbings, and explored the cemetery. We gathered by the entrance, and I collected the rubbings and crayons. Parents checked the cemetery to be sure we had not left any trash or disturbed anything before we walked back to school.

Debriefing and follow-up

Mingling among the students during the walk back to school, I picked up on their comments to one another and initiated some brief conversations, all to gauge their feelings. Back at school, I collected maps, data sheets, and clipboards and held an informal oral debriefing using such questions as these:

- What did you notice?
- Did the cemetery meet your expectations?
- Were you surprised by anything in particular?
- How did the cemetery compare to other cemeteries you have seen?
- What was the overall condition of the cemetery—did it need care?

Some students were inquisitive about the "old fashioned" names. Others expressed relief at finding that the cemetery was not a scary place after all. A few noted how this cemetery differed from the cemetery they had visited when a loved one had died. The discussion was helpful in other ways. Since it was very early in the school year, I was able to discover which students were comfortable expressing their opinions in front of the team and which ones were reticent.

Additionally, the discussion enlightened me about what students did not know, what they were interested in, and what I might highlight in the cemetery project during the year. For example, I could adjust activities to help students understand concepts involving past history and how it compared to the present. Students were then given a form, "Reflections on Our Visit to the Cemetery," as a homework assignment that posed half-a-dozen questions to elicit their feelings and opinions about the visit. These written answers and the discussions were types of formative assessment.

After the cemetery visit, there were several tasks to be accomplished. First, I sorted through the tombstone rubbings and discarded the ones that were illegible or badly torn. The remaining rubbings were prepared for display. Many of them were not centered on the newsprint, and the excess was trimmed with a paper cutter. The rubbings were then glued on different colors of construction paper for a fairly sturdy background that provided a nice contrast to the newsprint. Students or parent volunteers can assist in this task, but I did most of it myself the first year, so I would become familiar with the names of those buried in the cemetery.

The next day the mounted rubbings were displayed. Students liked searching for their rubbings and seeing all the different names. Our school hallway has strips for hanging student work above lockers, and this was a good place to hang the rubbings—especially since there were a lot of them. Later in the school year, when the students and I did presentations for parents and other groups, we displayed the rubbings on tables where they were eagerly examined by the audience.

Another task was to have students write thank you notes to those parents who attended and helped with the cemetery visit. A sheet of construction paper was folded in half with something simple like "THANK YOU…." on the cover and inside "for chaperoning our cemetery field trip." Students signed their names to each thank you note. The finished notes were dropped in manila envelopes, and students of the parents who had attended took them home. I tried to keep the process simple because we thanked parents many times throughout the year. Another type of thank you note was a photo from the field trip with students signing their names below it. This thank you required extra time, but was very popular with parents.

During our cemetery visit, students were unable to collect data from all the tombstones, so I asked for volunteers to go back to the cemetery after school for an hour on another day. Eight students readily agreed to participate and secured the necessary parent permission. I provided snacks for this hungry group, and then a parent and I drove the students to the cemetery. They really enjoyed our return to the cemetery to collect the remaining data and even wanted to do more tombstone rubbings.

Entering the data gathered

With the raw data collected, we were ready to develop an Excel spreadsheet. I typed the following headings and data from three tombstones into my classroom computer to get us started.

#	Side/Row/Letter	First Name	Last Name	Birth Year*	Death Year	Death Age	Months	Days
1	Left/5/A	Jim	Stewart	Not Given	1940	Not Given		
2	Left/5/B	Jerry	Sheeham	Not Given	1940	Not Given		
3	Left/5/C	Charles	Nelson	Not Given	1941	Not Given		

The headings can be explained as follows:

- "#" represents a counting of the number of people buried in the cemetery with tombstones.
- "Side/Row/Letter" indicates the left or right side of the cemetery, the row number, and the position in the row, e.g., A for the first one, B for the second one, etc.
- "Birth Year" is starred because it was computed by subtracting the death age in years from the death year. The lack of accuracy in doing this was a good discussion point for math class. Only one tombstone in the cemetery had a birth year given.
- Most of the tombstones have a "Death Age," but the ones above did not.
- The "Death Age" for babies buried in the cemetery is listed in "Months" and "Days" if that information appears on the tombstone.

With this beginning, several students with good computer skills entered the data before school each day using the data sheets from our trips. Most students were slow at entering data and found it tedious. As a result, I had to finish a few incomplete parts and check student accuracy. The wonderful thing about Excel is that data can be organized by any of the headings. This was most helpful because in our statistics unit various graphs worked best with the data sets organized in different ways. I had the school district print shop make copies for each way of organizing data—by cemetery location, last name, birth year, death year, and death age. With these data sheets completed, we were ready to begin our study of statistics.

Closing thoughts

No matter what the specifics of the study you are envisioning, it will likely follow much of the pattern and sequence we used. From this chapter, you could almost make a "to do" list that would include the various things to be done. While in the beginning you and your teammates will have to make most of the decisions and carry out the tasks, as soon as possible involve the students in the planning and conducting of the project. Ownership advances achievement.

CHAPTER

Statistics for a Math Unit and Beyond

Many people have asked me what a cemetery has to do with teaching math. Tombstones usually have birth and death dates and age at death, but those are not math problems; they are just numbers. There are other numbers, too, for the size of the cemetery and the trees in it. This chapter will show how to take these numbers and use them in a variety of ways to create interesting math problems that motivate students to learn important math processes, ones that relate directly to accepted national standards.

Incorporating math into the cemetery project began for my team with a statistics unit. During this unit, we made charts, drew a variety of graphs, and used graphing calculators to analyze and explore the tombstone data. I continued to use the math textbook and other activities that I had traditionally done, but substituted the cemetery data for textbook data. The blend worked well and students transitioned easily between the textbook and the cemetery activities.

The best part of using tombstone data was the discoveries we made about the people buried in the cemetery and the critical thinking students used to formulate questions from the data. The discoveries and questions flowed naturally into many social studies and language arts activities that are discussed in later chapters. The math became alive with references to these people and more connected to the real world. Students talked about them using the phrases "my person" or "my people" when analyzing data. There was a definite emotional connection when students found points on the graph that represented "their" people and how they compared to the others buried in the cemetery by death age and death year.

Throughout our work with the cemetery data, I found it important to stress the accuracy of the data and how it impacted our conclusions. First, data were only as good as what students copied down on the cemetery visit and entered into the computer. Second, data reflected the poor farm cemetery, not the poor farm itself. When people died at the poor farm, their families may have claimed their bodies and buried them elsewhere. We also had the problem of illegible tombstones that yielded no numbers. Any conclusions we reached from these data were incomplete because our data sample was incomplete, a common condition that needed to be understood and factored into conclusions.

Assessment for the following math activities was based on the chart or graph students made in class and often finished as homework. They received five points for a complete assignment and a partial score for incomplete or substantially incorrect work. Sometimes, students were asked to redo a graph or make changes to reinforce the correct way to do it. While students worked in class, I always circulated around the room and helped with making a chart or graph correctly. If students struggled with an activity, we revisited the topic the next day to strive for a better understanding.

The following activities used cemetery data rather than data provided in the text. They are sequenced like topics in the *Connected Math Series: Data About Us* (Dale Seymour Publications, 1998), which has topics comparable to most other middle school math textbooks.

Tombstone data chart

The textbook began the statistics unit by using the number of letters in students' names for a data set and making a frequency table with that information. We did this activity in class to practice organizing data, and then we used our tombstone data sheets that were organized by death year to organize the tombstone data. (See Appendix B, Tombstone Data Chart.) Students listed the years 1890 through 1941 vertically on a sheet of notebook paper. They counted four deaths for 1890 and recorded that number next to 1890 in a chart similar to that below.

Figure 4.1 Tombstone Data Chart

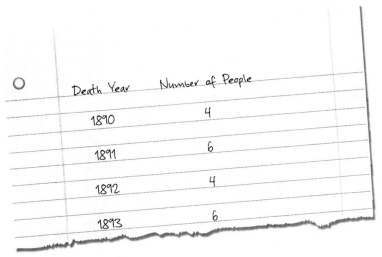

They were able to continue easily finding the frequency of deaths for each year. Rather quickly, however, students noted a problem. There were no deaths between 1912 and 1932. Why?

Everyone stopped counting, and we talked about possible reasons for no deaths in this time period. This was a teachable moment if there ever was one, and it provided an opportunity to work on the Communication Standard. Some students speculated that World War I had something to do with it. Other students proposed that the poor farm shut down during those years. One or two students thought no one died then. Several more guesses were offered. We were puzzled. Since I had recently found a local historian who had studied the cemetery, I suggested that we contact her to see if she could help us. The inquiry method was alive and well in our math class!

Students continued on with the chart, but ran into other problems. Three of the tombstones had death years that were illegible. Three other graves had missing tombstones. We talked about how to deal with these issues and concluded that the easiest way to handle the problem was to put an "Unknown" category below the last date, 1941. A worksheet for this activity that gives complete directions for organizing the tombstone data is Graphing and Charting Tombstone Data. (Appendix C)

Line plot

We discussed how to transfer these data from the chart to a line plot. Most students had made or at least seen a line plot before, so we only needed a quick review of what it looked like. It was obvious to some students that it would be difficult, if not foolish, to number every year from 1890 to 1940. Someone suggested grouping the years by decades.

With this in mind, students started the line plot by putting 42 Xs above the 1890s. The 1920s presented a problem because there were no data for that decade. Some students wanted to skip the decade entirely and not use it. This was a good opportunity to discuss with the class how we might resolve our dilemma. Most students realized the need to keep the 1920s in the line plot to maintain the same scale. We decided to finish the line plot using an "Unknown" column.

Figure 4.2 Line Plot for Tombstone Data

XXXXX

XXX

_____

1890s   1900s   1910s   1920s   1930s   1940s

Next, we looked at our line plot and talked about how impractical it was for this set of data. Students felt that it was cumbersome to make. We discussed what type of data set would be appropriate for a line plot. Additionally, if the line plot did not work with the cemetery data, what would? Students usually suggested a bar graph.

Bar graph

As with the line plot, students had previously made or seen bar graphs. The worksheet Graphing and Charting Tombstone Data shows the axes and the scale for a bar graph. (See Appendix C.) Actually, I thought it was a good learning experience for students to draw a bar graph on graph paper without the worksheet and use the tombstone data chart and the line plot they had already made. Some students had trouble with the scale for the number of people and used only those numbers that were found for a given year on the Y axis. This mistake provided a great opportunity to define scale and to figure out how to show it on a bar graph. Similar to the line plot, the graph included the 1920s and the "unknown" on the X axis. The size of the bar graph was not important as long as it fit on the paper.

Figure 4.3 Bar Graph for Death Years

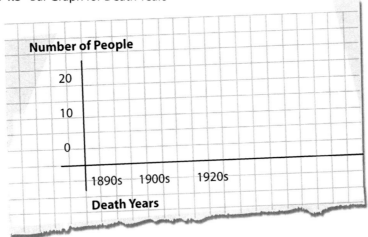

An emphasis on labeling the graph was important too. Each axis was supposed to be identified. If students were not familiar with the vocabulary of axis/axes and X/Y axis, this was a good time to introduce it or review it. The labels for identifying the axes were on charts already used or students could create their own labels. Providing a title for the bar graph was required, but the option of adding color was chosen by many students.

After the bar graphs were completed, it was enlightening for students to compare and discuss the finished graphs. Some students had horizontal graphs while others had vertical ones. Why? What scale did students choose to use for the number of people? Was there much variation within the class? This was also a good time to discuss mode and range if these terms were not already understood. The worksheet Graphing and Charting Tombstone Data, Appendix C, provides directions for frequency tables, line plots, and bar graphs.

Stem and Leaf Plot

Students were completely unfamiliar with a stem and leaf plot, so I introduced the basic setup of such a graph. A vertical line was drawn and the numbers 0 to 9, representing the tens unit, were placed to the left of the line. The ones digit of a number from the data was put on the right side across from its tens digit. If additional numbers had the same tens unit, the ones digit was placed next to the previous ones digit in the same row. After all the numbers were used, the plot was made again with the singles digits in order from smallest to largest. Students quickly learned how to make this graph. See Figure 4.4 for an example of our stem and leaf plot.

Figure 4.4 Stem and leaf plot showing death ages in years

```
0 | 00
1 |
2 | 7
3 | 25668
4 | 02368
5 | 0000111222458
6 | 0001123334556667899
7 | 0000000112223344455555666666788899
8 | 0012344556679
9 | 133348
```

Using data sheets for death ages, we made a stem and leaf plot. Immediately, students were puzzled by the number babies who died before they were one year old. After some discussion, the class decided to put 0 for the tens digits and 0 for the ones digit since this plot was based on years. Students easily recognized that they would have to number the left side up to 9 because we had 90-year-olds in the data. They then proceeded to go through the death years and place the single digits in the proper positions. Using these data made the problem longer than any problem from the math textbook, but students did not complain because it was meaningful to our cemetery study. The next step was for students to find the mode, median, and range. Finding the median for the cemetery data was difficult because there were so many numbers. Some students found the middle by counting the number of people, dividing by two, and counting that far into the graph. Others had learned a technique in an earlier grade of putting one finger on the first number and another finger on the last number in the plot and then moving their fingers into the plot simultaneously until they came to the middle number(s).

With our stem and leaf plots drawn, it was time to discuss them. I asked students what they thought about using this plot with the data. They liked the way so many numbers could be compacted into a relatively small area. They found it easy to find the mode, median, and range in this manner and thought it was a good graph to analyze data. Students were surprised that there were so many old people in the cemetery. They did not think that people lived that long in the late 1890s and early 1900s. Some questioned why there were no teenage deaths. Some students suggested that there were few or no such deaths at the poor farm because teenagers were able to work and would not need to live there. Class discussions were meaningful because the data had become more personal to students. I often heard them refer to the names of particular people whose tombstones they worked with and where they were located on the graph.

A back-to-back stem and leaf plot was an easy extension of our previous task. At open house one parent had asked me if there were more men or women buried in the cemetery. I did not know, but realized that this type of graph could easily show that information. In the graph the tens digits for death ages were written vertically from 0 to 9 with a line on both sides of the numbers. The ones digits for men were placed on one side and the ones digits for women were on the opposite side.

Figure 4.5 Back to Back Stem & Leaf Plot Of Death Ages for Men & Women

Women			Men
		0	
		1	
		2	7
		3	5668
60		4	238
8210		5	0011245
663		6	0001234556799
6422		7	000001334455566666788899
966553		8	001247
33		9	348

After giving students a brief introduction to a back-to-back stem and leaf plot (Figure 4.5), we went through the names and decided which people in the data were men and which were women. With the outdated names, I sometimes had to tell the students. In a few cases where we could not tell if it was a man or woman, we left that person out of the graph. Again, I cautioned that this omission did have an impact on the accuracy of our data and graph. On the completed graph, students quickly observed that there were more men than women. The median indicated that women had a slight advantage in terms of how long they lived while the mode favored the men.

Coordinate Graph

Because students were somewhat familiar with coordinate graphs, they were able to find points on a grid and draw a picture. My emphasis in introducing this graph was to compare two data sets. The previous graphs we had studied used only one set of data at a time. Comparing death years and death ages seemed to be a meaningful way to use the cemetery data in this type of graph. Perhaps we could find a significant year when many people died due to disease or a fire at the poor farm.

Before using the cemetery data to make a coordinate graph, I reviewed vocabulary: X and Y axis, origin, coordinates, ordered pair. For this unit, we were working only in the first quadrant. The most difficult part of making a coordinate graph for many students was figuring out the scale for numbering the death ages. I designed a worksheet, Comparing Death Years and Death Ages with a Coordinate Graph (Appendix D) to help students and directed them to label up to 1911 because this marked the gap in the data, and I felt it would be too tedious to include more points for later years. As it was, there were a large number of points for students to plot. We discussed what to do when there were two people who died in the same year at the same age. Some students put a circle around that dot while other students put two dots next to each other. As with the other graphs, a title was required and the axes needed labels. The complete directions for constructing such graphs are in Appendix D.

Figure 4. 6 Comparing Death Years and Death Ages on a Coordinate Graph

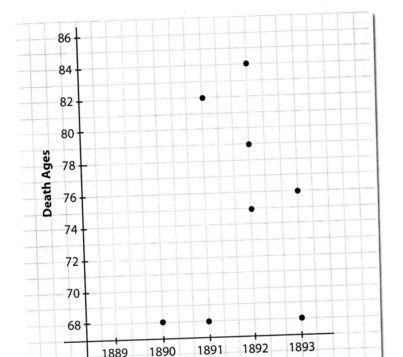

The next day we discussed the graph. Since we figured that the mode and median were 70 from the stem and leaf data, we drew a line across the graph at 70. We then looked for patterns. The students enjoyed talking about the graph and trying to analyze it. They were testing their critical thinking skills to explain the graph. Eventually the students decided they really could not see a pattern. We also talked about why the points should not be connected on this graph because each dot represented one person and that this type of coordinate graph was a scatter plot. One student surprised me by making the graph on her computer at home.

The activities of collecting tombstone data and creating graphs reflect expectations from the Data Analysis Math Standard. Students analyzed the data using the graphs, and during class we had extensive discussions about our data and the graphs. Students were spirited in coming up with inferences about irregularities in the data and making predictions as to why these irregularities existed.

Tombstone Data Project

During the second year of the project, I wanted students to do more writing about their graphs, for I realized that while they could make a graph, they didn't always really understand it. Writing forced them to think about their graph and also provided me a formative assessment of their understanding. The additional writing also related to the goals found in the Communication Standard.

I designed a Tombstone Data Project (Appendix E). Although we did most of the graphs in class, students often had to write about them as homework. When I collected and reviewed the finished packets, I was disappointed with the quality of the writing. I should have used more time to model how to prepare a well-written paragraph after we did the first one or two graphs and then followed up the next day with a discussion of their homework paragraphs.

Fractions, decimals, percents, and circle graphs

Cemetery data was useful in other math units besides statistics. A large part of the 6th grade curriculum covered fractions, decimals, and percents. I designed two activities that took the cemetery data and converted the number of deaths to percents. In the first activity students took the number of deaths in a decade and divided it by the total number of deaths to get a decimal. Multiplying that decimal by 100 converted it to a percent. The decimal multiplied by 360° in a circle calculated the degrees of the circle for the deaths in a decade. Students used an angle ruler to measure degrees and drew the graph on a sheet with a circle I provided. We practiced this activity first with easy problems from our textbook and then with cemetery data. See Appendix F for complete directions.

A second activity was similar, but a little more difficult. Students used the stem and leaf plot to find the number of deaths for each age group. As before, they found the decimal and the percent and drew a circle graph. This circle graph had many more sections than the first activity, but it did not seem to be a problem for students other than it took longer to draw. See Appendix G "Percent in a Circle Graph (Death Ages)."

These two activities relate to the Numbers and Operations Math Standard. Students were moving from data in fraction form to a decimal and then a percent. To make the graph, they computed with the decimal multiplied by 360°. An understanding of what these numbers meant was needed to correctly draw and label the graph.

Estimation

Several cemetery activities involved estimation, and we worked on it particularly when we took our second trip to the cemetery in the spring. During the school year we did not have a particular unit for estimation. It was incorporated into the curriculum as it related to a topic. For example, earlier, before doing a percent problem with calculations, we estimated an answer. Because we had just studied geometry in math class before our cemetery visit, activities also related to that topic.

In Cemetery Estimation, students put their arms around a tree and then made an educated guess about the circumference of the tree (For complete directions, see Appendix H.) With a partner they used a tape measure to find the actual circumference. Next, a pair of students estimated the height of the tree. To find the height, one student stood next to a tree, and the other student moved far enough away to count how many times the height of the student equaled the

Comparing an educated guess with an actual measurement was an enjoyable and meaningful math activity.

height of the tree. After measuring the height of the student, they multiplied the student height by the number of times the height of the student equaled the tree. This activity could also be completed back in the classroom using a photo of a student standing next to a tree.

In Cemetery Perimeter and Area, students were asked to estimate the length and width of the cemetery and then use those numbers to figure an estimated perimeter (See Appendix I). The cemetery was rectangular so this problem was easier than working with an irregular-shaped cemetery. I borrowed a measuring wheel from the physical education department, so students could actually measure the length and width and then calculate the perimeter. They enjoyed comparing their estimated answers with the answers based on measurement to find the amount of error. The length and width estimates and measurements were also used to predict and determine the area of the cemetery.

Estimation activities fell under three of the math standards. Our activities with the trees in the cemetery focused on the Measurement Standard. Finding the height of a tree used the height of a student as a common benchmark. A ratio was developed between the student height and the height of the tree. The scale factor was how many times the student height was equivalent to the height of the tree. This scale factor was multiplied by the student height to give an estimate for the height of the tree. In the circumference activity, students needed to accurately measure around the tree and compare it with their estimate. Finding the perimeter and area of the cemetery correlated to the Geometry Standard. Fluent computation and reasonable estimates that were needed for the above activities correlated to the Number and Operations Standard.

Graphing calculators

Graphing calculators are not required for a cemetery project, but they are a wonderful tool. The calculators were used to enrich our study of data and did not replace traditional methods of working with data. Students who struggled in math became more engaged in our study when the calculators were used.

I purchased TI73 graphing calculators because they were considered appropriate for upper elementary/middle school students and were easy to use in making various statistical graphs. The students, with a few exceptions, loved using them. A few students panicked when they could not find certain keys or they simply pushed the wrong button. Initially, it was rather exhausting to do both a group lesson on the graphing calculators and assist individual students who were behind or lost. I did have a teacher calculator on my overhead projector so students could at least see what should be on their screen. Ideally, it would be helpful to have another person who is familiar with the calculator to assist the first few times students use them, or perhaps have students work in pairs to help one another.

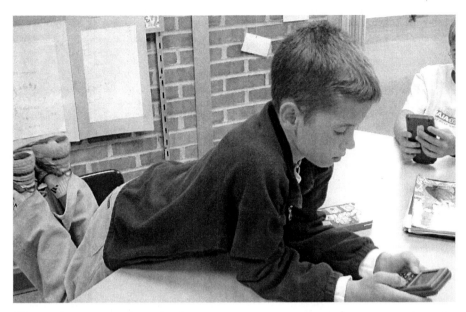

Students quickly took to the new graphing calculators, which made it possible for them to create impressive graphs.

Students were not fluent with the calculators in the beginning, so I needed to introduce them before we could do any cemetery graphs. I numbered the calculators and each student was assigned a particular number. The calculators were stored in a wall hanging with numbered pouches. At the end of class, I could easily glance at the wall hanging to see if all the calculators had been returned. The high cost of these calculators made their security important.

The first lesson started with showing students a few basic keys and giving them time to explore the calculator on their own and to share with the class what they discovered. Exploration time was important so students could gain a comfort level with them. Since we were doing exponents in prime factorizations during a factors/multiples unit, I showed them how to use the calculator to find the answer to an exponent problem. We compared solving exponent problems on the graphing calculator to any scientific calculators that students owned. Textbook problems and worksheets were used to give students practice material. The lesson was effective and helped students become familiar with the layout of this digital tool.

After completing the cemetery graphs on paper as previously described, we used the graphing calculators to enter the tombstone data for deaths by decades. By pressing the "List" button we came up with a chart with columns. In List 1 we placed vertically the years 1890 through 1940. In List 2 we typed in the frequency of deaths for a decade

The next step was setting up the requirements for the graph. By pressing "2nd" and then "Y=" we came to the stat plots screen. We only needed "Plot 1" so we proceeded to that screen by pushing "enter" and turned it "on." The type of graph now had to be selected. Students experimented with choosing different graphs to reflect our data. They really enjoyed such exploring and sharing their discoveries with the class.

During the unit on fractions, decimals, and percents, we drew the death by decades circle graph previously described and then created it on the graphing calculators. We entered the same decades and frequency data into "List" as used for the line plot and returned to "Plot 1" to make the circle graph. We looked at the graph with numbers identified (how many people died in a particular decade) and then with percents. This activity was a good review of what we had done with the paper graph. We did not do a death age and frequency graph because it was more complicated, and there was not sufficient time.

Survey results

At the end of the statistics unit students filled out a "Statistics Unit Survey" consisting of just four short answer questions that would assess students' attitudes on using cemetery data for the unit (See Appendix J). A few students mentioned some of the problems being too long. They were referring to the coordinate graph problem on death years which took much longer to make than I had anticipated. Using fewer people from the data to make the graph would have been more appropriate. Otherwise, students were overwhelmingly positive about working with the cemetery data. Typical comments from the survey were:

- I got to organize real data.
- It made me listen because it was interesting.
- I really love the graphing calculators.
- I think they (the calculators) are very handy and fun to use.
- Learning about statistics was made fun.
- It was exciting to learn about the people buried there.
- It was making me learn a lot.
- I love making graphs.
- It taught me more than I knew.
- It is something that actually happened.

Conclusion

The math for the cemetery project was easily woven into the regular 6th grade math curriculum. Tombstone data graphs were part of a textbook statistics unit. Although graphing calculators were not part of the textbook unit, they greatly enhanced our study and added a technology component. Percent graphs with cemetery data were inserted into the study of fractions, decimals, and percents. Since estimation occurs throughout the math and science curriculum during the school year, the tree estimation activities were timely and appropriate when we visited the cemetery.

During the first year of the project, students did not complete a special cemetery assessment. Graphs and charts counted for five points as did the regular class work and homework assignments. I found it important to give students as much time as possible to work on graphs in class so I could monitor their progress, especially the beginning steps of setting up a graph. During and after class I evaluated student performance and identified topics I might need to review with the class. Students with learning disabilities were sometimes given altered assignments when the information for a graph was considerable.

During the second year, I used the Tombstone Data Project (Appendix E) as an assessment for cemetery statistics. Students compiled their graphs along with short paragraphs in a report that I collected and graded. The quality of the student writing led me to spend more time in the future modeling such writing and having students share and discuss their writing more. Such exercises would be coordinated with the Language Arts teacher in a team.

Using the cemetery and the tombstone data for math activities and the statistics unit was a big success. We studied the entire required math curriculum and more. Students were motivated and seemed to enjoy working with data that represented real people. When we found discrepancies in the data, such as no tombstone data for the 1920s, students' curiosity was aroused and we had terrific discussions on possible reasons.

This success in advancing the math achievement of our students enabled me to meet the Toyota TIME Grant goal of performance in 6th grade math. Our students' growth was demonstrated by the scores on the standardized tests that took place in the spring. Likewise, the promotion of positive students attitude toward math was equally successful as shown by comparing the Math Attitude Survey filled out at the beginning of the school year with the one completed at the end. The results, along with the many comments students made, unquestionably indicated that a positive change in attitude towards math had occurred. The math activities in the cemetery project had made math more "real," active, and connected to other subject areas and to the community.

The math of the tombstone data and the student analysis and evaluation of it produced many questions. Students were curious and wanted to find answers. This was the point at which we delved into social studies to pursue the history of the cemetery, the poor farm, and the community. The Connections Standard for math was addressed in this relationship to social studies as well as in other areas. All in all, the math aspect of the cemetery project proved to be a solid success.

CHAPTER

Questions and Answers from Social Studies

When the planning of the cemetery project began, I knew exactly how it would fit with the math curriculum and the related national standards. Yet, I had little idea how to incorporate a social studies component. The history of the poor farm and the local community were obvious areas of content to study, but in what way? Since the school year began with the math component of the project, I had ample time to figure out the next part of the plan. Brainstorming with my team teacher, other teachers, neighbors, and family was helpful. Contacting the county historical society also proved to be a good idea. As a result, the social studies portion of the cemetery project evolved in several surprising ways—ways that were ideal for meeting both developmental and academic needs of students.

Having found his name and contact information on the county website, I called the president of the Ingham County Historical Commission in September. At the close of our conversation, he invited the students and me to an evening commission meeting in early October to talk about our project. I informed my students and asked for volunteers to attend with me. Seven students returned permission slips, so my husband and I drove them to the county courthouse. (After that, I added a sentence on the permission slips asking if parents were willing to drive.) Throughout the year, there were many after school project-related opportunities like this in which students and parents could participate. I was always amazed by which students chose to do certain activities on their own time. An activity sometimes attracted a diverse group of students, providing a form of differentiation that I had not expected.

Prior to the commission meeting, the students and I discussed how we would present our project to the commissioners. I was delighted at the enthusiasm and willingness of these sixth graders to talk to people they did not know in a place they had never been! We identified topics that they might share with the commissioners: our cemetery visit, tombstone rubbings, collecting data from the tombstones, and the math evaluation of the data. Each topic was quickly claimed by a student, with some students choosing to say nothing. We took several rubbings, the list of data derived from the tombstones, a poster of photos, and our beginning math activities.

Our visit to the courthouse started with a brief tour led by one of the commissioners. We walked by a showcase that contained a county historical marker, and the commissioner suggested that we might apply for such a marker if the cemetery was over one hundred years old. We would have to fill out an application form and show proof to the commission that the cemetery was worthy of such an honor. There was also an application fee that we would have to pay. At that moment, I realized securing a marker for the cemetery would be a terrific end-of-the-school-year activity. Our team could strive for obtaining an official historical marker rather than simply putting up a sign to identify the cemetery. The students seemed very interested in working toward such a goal.

We crammed into a small room where the commission met. I began with a brief overview of the cemetery project and how it started with a Toyota Time Grant. Next, the students took over and talked about each of the topics they had selected. I was pleased at how well they did and the enthusiasm with which they spoke. The commissioners seemed impressed and gave us several suggestions for activities such as checking for Civil War veterans who qualified for special tombstones and studying the large old trees in the cemetery.

The next day students shared their experience at the Historical Commission meeting with the rest of the team. They explained how to obtain a historical marker for the cemetery and the team enthusiastically agreed that we should acquire one. (That process is described in Chapter 8). One student told how her parents had gotten a historical marker for an old schoolhouse on the family property, and a few weeks later her mom brought in the marker to show the class. The practice of students sharing their experiences and reflections with the whole team after any mini-field trip became a tradition for the duration of the school year. It was a powerful learning experience for all to have students, now serving as teachers, share their adventures and discoveries with interested learners.

A new resource emerges

We finished the math statistics unit in October, but with many unanswered questions on our minds. We wanted to figure why our tombstone data did not always make sense. One of my neighbors told me about a research historian in our community who had studied the cemetery and even recorded all the tombstone information twenty-five years earlier. Would this person be helpful in our quest for answers?

We were most fortunate that I was able to find that person, Mrs. Elaine Davis. She was a valuable resource who worked with us throughout the year and participated again the following year with a new group of students. Mrs. Davis was astonished and pleased that anyone would be interested in studying a cemetery the way we did, especially a group of middle school students. When I met with Mrs. Davis, I knew we needed her to come and talk with the students. I invited her to present a brief history of our community, describe a poor farm and the cemetery's connection to it, explain what resources she used in her historical studies, and tell how she became interested in this field of study. Additionally, I shared with her our questions about the data that had surfaced in math class. (Throughout the cemetery project I found it important to give guest speakers specific information about what they should speak on and the amount of time available for their presentations.)

Mrs. Davis did an excellent job talking with the students, who listened intently. She spoke for about 20 minutes weaving the history of the community with that of the poor farm. She pointed out that our cemetery data did not represent all poor farm inhabitants because some former residents had been buried elsewhere by relatives or friends. She also gave possible explanations for the inconsistencies in our data. She said that during the time period that the cemetery had no tombstones, some bodies were likely to have been sent to the University of Michigan for medical students to study. Another possibility was that lacking money, some people were buried without tombstones. She further indicated that the cemetery may have had so many elderly people because they outlived their families or resources.

When Mrs. Davis finished her opening remarks, students flooded her with questions. In describing the poor farm, she happened to mention some of the diseases that were common at that time. Students were fascinated in hearing about smallpox, whooping cough, and other diseases that they were unfamiliar with, and they wanted to know more about them—another line of study that could be pursued and another service learning possibility. It was exciting to witness the enthusiasm of students as they asked questions about the history of the poor farm and the era in which it existed. New learning was taking place.

A mini field trip

With the help and encouragement of Mrs. Davis, I made arrangements to take a small group of students to the Library of Michigan to conduct research on the poor farm and its cemetery. Because I had never been to the Library of Michigan that was located in nearby Lansing, I made an appointment with the librarian in the local history and genealogy section to learn my way around first before taking the students. There were so many materials available to study that I drew a map of the area to help me remember where everything was located. For teachers working on such a project, access to such a large library may not be possible, but area colleges will also contain research resources in their libraries. Furthermore, vast amounts of historical and genealogical material can now be accessed on the Internet and students can do the research. Another option to consider is the growing number of counties that have historical societies with extensive collections, including microfilmed newspapers. There may even be a previous record of tombstone data from a cemetery which students could cross-check with their data.

Since the entire team was too large to visit the library, I asked for volunteers to go after school. Eleven students returned permission slips, and so a mother and I drove them there. We met the librarian who knew we were coming, and she showed us how to use our own names to do coding for census materials. Students learned that this code is also the number on a person's driver's license. The librarian took the students on a tour of this section of the library and showed them materials they might use in future visits to research the poor farm and the cemetery, including boxes of microfilm with the census index and census data.

The census is one of the best ways to explore genealogy, although the federal government keeps the information private for seventy-two years. At the time we did our project, the 1930 census was the last one available to the public. We spent more than an hour at the library before leaving to return students to their homes. The following day we wrote a thank you note to the parent who participated and to the librarian in Lansing. As usual the students reported on our activities to all. Again it was evident that they had learned much.

Publicity for the project

In February I got a call from a local newspaper reporter who had heard about the cemetery project and wanted to do a story. Unfortunately, there were no specific cemetery activities planned for the day the newspaper people wanted to interview us and take pictures. However, I had students use the graphing calculators for a non-cemetery math lesson we were doing. The photographer was happy taking pictures of the engaged and confident students using these new digital tools. In a classroom across the hall, I set up a display of the different cemetery artifacts students had made and activities that they had done thus far in the school year. When the photographer was done, and the reporter had interviewed several students about using the graphic calculators, I took our visitors across the hall to see the display and talk with several different students about other aspects of the project.

The reporter requested permission to put my e-mail address in the newspaper article so anyone with information about the cemetery could contact me. It turned out to be a great idea because I heard from a former administrator of the medical care facility from which the poor farm had evolved. As we studied the cemetery and received more and more publicity, many individuals would contact me with their stories about the poor farm or its residents, which I shared with students. These tidbits of information were helpful in developing a mental picture of the poor farm and how it evolved into a hospital and then into a medical care and rehabilitation facility.

Gathering census data

A few students and I took another after-school trip to the Library of Michigan in March to focus on using census records to learn about poor farm residents. As usual, I described the purpose of the mini field trip and asked for volunteers. Some students who turned in a slip had gone on the previous trip while others had not. We ended up with seven students, a good number because the microfilm and copy machines were limited. Fortunately, Mrs. Davis volunteered to be there and help us at the library.

When using the census records, we started with the index to look up on microfilm the last name of the head of the household in a particular census year and state based on the code we had learned on our last visit. The index gave information to find the actual box of census microfilm we wanted. The poor farm, however, was a special case because residents were listed under the name of the administrator, whom we did not know. Instead, we went directly to the census microfilm for a given year in Michigan and looked through it for Meridian Township, where our cemetery is located. Mrs. Davis showed us how to use the microfilm machines, and when we found the record of poor farm residents for a given census, we learned how to use copy machines to make a paper copy from the microfilm. We collected the census records for 1880 and 1900 through 1930. Since our project began, however, websites like heritagequestonline.com and Ancestry.com are available on the Internet so students can do this kind of research if the school or public library has a subscription to these sites.

Reading the census materials we copied was a challenge. They were handwritten, and the microfilm was sometimes in poor condition. I picked the 1900 Census for us to work on in class because it was the easiest to read and made multiple copies for the whole team. During team time I passed out the census with the tombstone data list organized alphabetically—with magnifying glasses since the writing was small. Students were excited seeing names of people they recognized from the cemetery tombstones. Personal information such as date and place of birth, citizenship, education, and more was included about the people in this particular census. Students copied data from the census to a form prepared by the Library of Michigan which was much easier to read. They were not only learning about the people in our cemetery, but realizing what a census was and the significance of using it for research.

Tributes received

As the result of a letter writing activity described in the next chapter, I received a call from the office of State Legislator Gretchen Whitmer. The secretary indicated that Representative Whitmer wanted to visit our team and present the students with a tribute from the legislature for our work with the cemetery. We agreed on a day in April when Mrs. Whitmer could come to our school. The students volunteered to do a presentation for her and our school principal on the various activities we had accomplished. Mrs. Whitmer asked many good questions, and students responded enthusiastically with excellent answers. After the students were finished, Representative Whitmer presented the framed tribute to the team. She then took time to talk about her job as a legislator and to explain her reasons for becoming involved in state government; she then recommended that students consider public service in their futures.

Several months later in the summer when I attended one of the meetings of the Ingham County Board of Commissioners, we received another framed tribute. Their formal resolution honoring the team concluded with commending the team and their teachers for "unlocking the history behind the Ingham County Poor Farm and the Ingham County Home Cemetery." It is interesting to note that while the project was initially based on mathematics, in the long run activities that were focused on other areas became the sources of many of the important learnings and understandings gained from the project.

Another mini field trip

In May several students and I took another after-school trip to the Library of Michigan where we again met Mrs. Davis. Our goal this time was to find and copy information about the poor farm and its residents from old local newspapers on microfilm. Newspaper obituaries would normally be quite helpful and easy to find because the death date would be available from the tombstone information. However, people buried in the poor farm cemetery usually did not have obituaries. When they died, their families chose not to claim the bodies for burial, or there was no family left to prepare an obituary. Occasionally, there might be a small notice in the newspaper about someone who died at the "county home" in the local news, but those references were random and difficult to find.

Consequently, students had to rely on an annual report by the poor farm superintendent that was published in the newspaper. These reports often listed disbursements made, an inventory of farm products and livestock on hand, a list of "inmates" at the poor farm, and the number of days they resided there. As students looked through the newspapers using the microfilm machines, they ran across other articles referring to the poor farm that ranged from a notice about an addition to the poor farm to one inmate causing the death of another inmate through carelessness. Students were quite captivated by these newspapers that were so different from our newspapers. Advertisements and "old language" particularly caught their attention. We copied all the pages about the poor farm that we could find and shared them with the team the next day. Everyone was intrigued with these old newspapers and with the unusual references to the poor farm they included.

A sidelight emerges

There was one clear exception to inmates at the poor farm dying unknown and forgotten. J.B. Walker was locally famous for his paper cuttings. He often did intricate cut-outs that he sent to acquaintances. In the 1980s the museum at Michigan State University did a special exhibit of his work and a book of his cuttings was published *(Your Wellwisher, J.B. Walker)*. One of the physical education teachers at our school was familiar with paper cutting. She came to our class and demonstrated it for students. After showing how it was done, she gave students a chance to try it. In the days following a number of students continued to experiment with this interesting form of art. (This was just one of many brief enrichment experiences that came about during the project.) Students also enjoyed hearing about research that Mrs. Davis had done on Walker's life. He lived at the poor farm because he had many debts and couldn't get along with his family. Several old newspaper articles described legal action between his sons and him. When he died, however, his family claimed his body, and he was buried in the family plot in an unmarked grave at another cemetery in the area. Students were fascinated with J.B. Walker, and every time we did a presentation, they always had to tell about him.

Most of the cemetery-based social studies activities were done apart from the regular social studies class taught by my partner. They were done during homeroom, team time, or after school with mini field trips. The team time was created when the daily schedule was rearranged by assemblies, standardized testing, or special events. On some occasions, academic classes were shortened by 10 minutes to get the time. During these different activities I used informal assessments to help design further activities based on observing students doing research, sharing their results with the rest of the team, and team discussion.

The cemetery offered many opportunities for activities that addressed the social studies standards. For instance, Culture and the Five Themes of Geography proposed by the National Council for Social Studies are big components in our school district's 6th grade curriculum, and the cemetery and poor farm are ties to a different era for the local community that could be compared and contrasted with current culture and the geography theme of place. The presentation by Mrs. Davis and her discussion with students highlighted the differences between the poor farm era and the present. Old newspapers exhibited a very visual difference in the culture.

The inquiry method of selecting main questions to investigate certainly lent itself to the research we accomplished. Questions such as "How has our community changed since 1900?" or "What does a cemetery study tell us about our community and its values?" can help focus research. Individual and group research projects could be developed for students to investigate such topics. Researching individuals buried in a cemetery allowed students to develop a sense of historical perspective and to understand how the world has changed since earlier times. This perspective meets the standards theme of Time, Continuity, and Change.

If the cemetery is connected to a church, a poor farm, or some other institution, the theme of Individuals, Groups, and Institutions can be explored. When my students attended a county Historical Commission meeting, presented to a state legislator, and received tributes from the state legislature and the county commission, they were interacting with forms of government as described by the Power, Authority, and Governance themes. Global Connections could be studied through the nationalities of people buried in the cemetery; students could research reasons that different nationalities might be represented or, conversely, why little ethnic diversity might be found. A particular cemetery chosen for study can relate to other standards in unique ways as did our poor farm cemetery.

The lessons related to social studies in the poor farm cemetery turned out to be quite different than anything I might have planned. We started out simply trying to learn whatever we could about the cemetery and the poor farm based upon the many questions that came out of our study of the tombstone data in math. The willingness of a local historian to share her expertise and to teach the students about research methods using primary sources at the Library of Michigan was an incredible experience for the students and me. Our questions from math were answered, or reasonable explanations were suggested, and we learned a lot about our community history in the process. The cemetery project proved to be rich in possibilities for engaging young adolescents in learning many important social studies concepts and skills.

CHAPTER

Effective Communication in Language Arts: Then & Now

Language arts inevitably are involved in any educational activity, and a cemetery project is certainly no exception. In this project we carried out a number of activities that focused on major aspects of language arts beyond the ongoing, routine reading and writing tasks. These activities were all aligned with the NCTE/IRA standards. Other potentially fruitful activities presented themselves that we were unable to pursue for lack of time. In this chapter we will describe some of the activities we did that were primarily language arts-focused and identify other possibilities.

Putting the three R's to use

Prior to visiting the cemetery, students filled out a survey that gave me valuable information as to their comfort level with being in a cemetery. This was a task that forced them to write about their thoughts and feelings. For some 6th graders it was difficult to write or talk about something so abstract, and this gave them an opportunity to struggle with this type of writing. Beyond just visiting the cemetery, such a project offers many possibilities for meaningful writing and discussion about death and one's feelings towards it. The way different cultures deal with death and burial offers additional topics to explore, especially when a team is composed of culturally diverse students. The project offers an impersonal entry point for discussions to occur.

As we progressed through the different types of graphs using tombstone data, students evaluated the graphs to see if they were appropriate for the data we had. They looked for patterns and generated questions when some aspect of the data did not make sense. They described verbally and in writing the patterns they found or the lack of them. The class discussions were spirited, and the students eagerly suggested reasons for the kind of results we were getting. During this math-based unit, students were unaware of how much "language arts" they were doing.

The social studies activities described in the previous chapter likewise called for mastering many language arts skills. Students researched the poor farm and the people who resided there through a variety of resources. Besides learning how to access information, they had to read and interpret special materials such as census data and old newspapers. Each time a small group made a trip to the Library of Michigan, these students returned with copies of what they had found and shared them with the rest of the team. They had to explain what they had done and the significance of their discoveries to the satisfaction of their peers.

When students participated in the many presentations we did about the cemetery project, they had to plan their remarks to effectively communicate with the particular audience at hand. Speaking to a newspaper reporter who knew nothing about our project differed from a presentation to parents who already had considerable knowledge about it. The student presentation to the county Historical Commission involved making a persuasive argument for issuing the cemetery a historical marker. Students found that they were more comfortable speaking in front of a group if they had a few specific points in mind and had an object to hold that was related to their comments, something to occupy their hands.

The activities above directly represented many of the standards for language arts—even though they were not done in a language arts class. Students used different forms of language to communicate (writing and speaking) with different audiences (e.g. our team, individuals and groups outside the school) and for different reasons (e.g. to inform the team about research, to make an argument for a historical marker). Reading newspapers from the 1900s exposed students to working with a medium produced in another era with unusual vocabulary and a different format. Likewise, research at the Library of Michigan introduced students to new resources for acquiring information.

My team teacher directed an activity involving the cemetery during a unit on letter writing in her language arts class. Students worked in small groups to prepare a letter describing the project that would go to individuals of note in the school district, community, and state. A list of such people with addresses was distributed and the names were divided among the groups. Students learned proper formatting for such a letter. They also considered possible topics on which to write: a description of our team and school, the cemetery project itself, and some of the specific activities that we did. Students wrote and revised their letters in order to have one that communicated effectively and, of course, was grammatically correct. The assessment of these letters was based on the 6th grade standards for grammar and related areas.

Many of the people who received these letters responded with their own letters and, in a few cases, by e-mail. Students were thrilled to receive feedback and enjoyed sharing it. Most of the response letters were on letterhead paper, which was a new format for some students. This provided an opportunity to consider letterheads, who uses them, and why, and to examine some samples.

A few students created their own letterheads. The most important response was the one received from State Representative Whitmer, who indicated she planned to come visit our classroom and present the team with a tribute from the state legislature signed by the Governor.

Other language arts opportunities

There are more possible activities built around language arts in a cemetery project than any one class or group could ever complete. One time-proven activity is to draw on the entertaining *Spoon River Anthology* (1915) by Edgar Lee Masters. This famous collection of interesting, free-form poems or epitaphs by dead characters from the fictional town of Spoon River makes for enjoyable reading by students. Students are fascinated by these colorful people and how they describe their life, their death, or just the complaints they have about the way their grave is being treated.

A follow-up to reading in this anthology would be for students to create an epitaph. Students could write their own epitaph, one for a relative, someone in the cemetery based on research, or a purely fictional one. Having students stand by a tombstone, recite a factual epitaph for the person buried there, and perhaps dress in a period costume, would be the basis for a community event, possibly a meaningful addition to a community's celebration or anniversary of some sort. See http://www.uhigh.ilstu.edu/laptops/promisingpractices/englishcollaboration. pdf for the story of an annual Evergreen Cemetery Discovery Walk that uses laptop technology, wikispace, and a cemetery walk-through to advance creative writing. While done with high school students, it offers many ideas that can be adapted.

Some language arts activities in a project may be shaped by a special association that the cemetery has with another organization, as we had with the local historical society. Then again, some may come in unannounced. Some days after one of our presentations, someone who had been in the audience sent me two poems by Will Carleton, a poet laureate of Michigan, who died in 1912. Poems such as these, "Over the Hill to the Poor-House" and "Over the Hill from The Poor-House," could be shared with students. They could provide students with an opportunity to gain an appreciation of poetry and to practice the effective oral reading of poetry. Indeed, Will Carleton's poor-house poems brought him national recognition. Carleton's legacy shows us that history is made through the simple events of our "ordinary" lives full of monotony, grief, and joy and by sharing his intimate knowledge of the plight of the aged and of those with indifferent or no families. (The poem, "Over the Hill to the Poor-House is in Appendix K.) Students might also investigate and identify other poems like these to examine poetry from past eras, the topics included in them, and their differences from today's vocabulary. A cemetery, incidentally, makes an excellent venue for writing poetry. Its ambience supports reflection and creativity. Share a Robert Frost poem or two or even the last stanza of William Cullen Bryant's "Thanatopsis" with the group; then let individuals find a spot to quietly compose some free verse or rhymed poems.

Students could also read a novel set in the time when the cemetery was most actively in use and in an essay compare the era in the book with our current culture or compare the novel with a modern novel they have read. Designing a book jacket, writing a short story using the same time period, or creating a poster describing the action in the story are other possibilities.

There are many outlets for students to "publish" a story on a cemetery project. If the team has a weekly or monthly newsletter, students could provide stories about project activities for it. Articles for the school newspaper and the local newspaper are always open opportunities. Some students might enjoy working on a PowerPoint that could be shared with other classes or be a part of an exchange with students in another country. Others could develop a website with stories and pictures from activities or update part of a school website. Podcasts from a website would give students an audio variation for reporting project activities.

Summary

A cemetery-based study offers many possibilities for language arts activities throughout a project and for creative end products that are shared with others. Such studies also lend themselves easily to differentiation, small group work, and the incorporation of various forms of technology. The national standards can easily be addressed with cemetery activities directed toward reading a variety of texts and writing with a range of strategies for different audiences and purposes.

From Tombstones to Maps...
Science in the Cemetery

During the school year our entire team made two trips to the cemetery for the project. In the fall we focused on collecting tombstone data and doing rubbings. The death dates and the death ages provided the data for the statistics unit in math. The names on the tombstones, in addition to the statistical data, gave us information for the historical studies that evolved.

The spring trip was completely different. We concentrated on science and math activities involving weathering, mapping, measurement, and estimation. This trip followed the classroom study of rocks and minerals. Unfortunately, our cemetery was not a good choice for studying a variety of rocks. There are one hundred six marble tombstones, one granite tombstone, and thirty-three flat cement markers. However, students wanted to return to "our" cemetery rather than going to a different one with a greater selection of tombstone rock.

During our study of rocks and minerals we had discussed weathering and had done experiments related to it. The cemetery provided a good science lab for this topic. Students could look at marble tombstones from the 1890s and see how weathered they were in comparison to marble tombstones from twenty years later. The names on the earlier ones could rarely be read while the later ones were legible, but showing some weathering.

The marble tombstones could not be compared to the cement markers because the latter were placed much later and were lying flat on the ground. A good question that students thought about was which type of tombstone would have the greater weathering if they were made of the same material, the upright or flat? The one granite tombstone with a death year of 1911 was in excellent condition. If the tombstone actually dated back to that time, it was withstanding weathering very well.

We only discussed our tombstone observations. I did not create a worksheet because we needed the time for other activities. Otherwise, this would have been an opportunity for students to write about their observations, create questions, and suggest answers about tombstone weathering. It would be interesting to take close-up pictures of several tombstones at the beginning of the year and then pictures of the same tombstones a year later to see if the effects of weathering would be apparent in just one year.

Another issue that affects tombstone weathering and is open to student inquiry is air pollution. In the classroom we had done activities simulating the effects of acid rain and other pollutants on chalk. Students questioned to what degree the tombstones in the cemetery were weathered by pollution and whether a cemetery in a different location might be more or less impacted by air pollution. Would tombstones in a city cemetery be more weathered than those in a rural cemetery where there would be fewer industrial plants and traffic?

Using the content standard for science as inquiry would certainly lead to a lot of possibilities in the cemetery on just weathering. Other standard based learning appropriate for 6th grade curriculum fell under earth science. When students observed the sediment from the tombstones falling to the ground and mixing with the dirt and grass, they were seeing weathering as a destructive force and how that leads to the formation of soil. Conversely, looking for tombstones with crystals would emphasize the constructive forces that formed these tombstones. Since we grew crystals in the science classroom during our mineral study, students could link that experience with the crystals they observed in the marble and granite tombstones.

In a cemetery with more variety of tombstone rock, or even with our limited selection, a good inquiry question for students is: "Which is the best rock to use for a tombstone?" A worksheet with directions and a chart was used to list different tombstones, evaluate the type of rock, and rate the condition of the tombstone with respect to weathering. See Appendix L, Tombstone Geology Activity and Appendix M, Tombstone Chart. The chart portion of Tombstone Geology could be used as an assessment measure with students receiving points for each section or row completed. While the students are working on the assignment in the cemetery, a teacher could visually evaluate how easily they are able to identify rock type and how much they have to rely on labeled rock samples for identification.

Since our cemetery was limited in the type of rocks, I chose to spend more time on students mapping the cemetery, which was the introductory part of our landform unit. The initial goal was to have students simply sketch a map of the basic features of the cemetery and include a compass rose, a key with symbols, and a title. The Cemetery Map Rubric was a guideline for them to follow in making the map (See Appendix N). Students drew a rough draft at the cemetery and the next day they used class time to work on a final copy that would be graded according to the rubric. The map was homework if extra time was needed to finish it. Large paper, 17 x 11, was used so it would be easier to draw for students whose fine motor skills had not fully developed. A student map of the cemetery is found in Appendix O.

I wanted to have students draw topographic maps of the cemetery when we studied them in class a few weeks later. Instead of returning to the cemetery with the whole class, I had planned to take a few student volunteers to the cemetery after school with GPS units to get elevation readings for use in drawing a map. Our cemetery does have some elevation change, particularly in one corner, but it lacks the dramatic elevation changes another cemetery might have. Unfortunately, it was near the end of the school year and we did not have the opportunity to make a topographic map.

Biology teachers would have a different focus if they participated in a cemetery project. If the cemetery has a number of trees or is bordered by a wooded area, tree identification and estimating tree height and circumference are possible activities. If there are very large trees, students could try to determine the ages of the trees and whether there is a correlation with the age of the cemetery.

Identifying the plants and bushes within the cemetery and along the outside edges is an obvious option as well. Since our cemetery had poison ivy outside the fence, there was a teachable moment to learn about that infamous plant. Looking for signs of animal life and considering the whole concept of a habitat would be a possibility, especially if the cemetery is located in a more rural area. In the winter, the snow-covered cemetery might be an undisturbed area filled with animal tracks waiting to be identified.

With a chemistry and earth science curriculum, I focused on weathering, rock types, and mapping, but a cemetery holds learning opportunities for any type of science. It offers a laboratory where the inquiry method can be implemented. Skills of observation, inference, and experimentation enable students to ask questions about what they see or what they do not see in the cemetery. These questions can lead students to collect data and to think critically about the relationships between their evidence and possible explanations. The conditions in a particular cemetery may determine the direction inquiry will take in that setting, but opportunities always exist.

CHAPTER

Service Learning–
Make a Difference!

Service learning may not be an academic subject, but it has real importance and has rightfully gained acceptance as a component of the middle school curriculum. It provides young adolescents with experiences that have inherent worth and importance. Service learning instills the value of participating in the well-being of the community and giving back to it. In some ways, it is an extension of social studies and the democratic idea of maintaining the common good. Many school systems, even one state, require a certain number of hours of community service to graduate from high school. The National Honor Society recognizes the value of service learning by requiring scholastically able students to earn a number of community service hours for membership.

Middle schools, of course, have always engaged in service projects. In my school these projects have ranged from a school-wide food drive to a team buying Christmas presents for a needy family. I taught an exploratory class called Helping Hands and just a few of our activities included playing Bingo with seniors in a nursing home, reading to pre-school children in daycare, raising money with a bake sale to buy a llama through Heifer International, and making Valentines for Veterans. Service learning as now conceived, however, is not an isolated event, but a curriculum component that is closely tied to the academic program. One major goal of middle level education set forth in *This We Believe* (NMSA, 2010) all but requires students to experience service learning activities, namely: "Understand local, national, and global civic responsibilities and demonstrate active citizenship through participation in endeavors that serve and benefit those larger communities." (p.12)

Service learning opportunities emerge

With our cemetery project, the notion of providing some service came up early. Towards the end of our first visit, unsolicited student comments offered suggestions about ways we could improve the cemetery. Since the poor farm cemetery had been rather neglected, numerous possibilities for improvement were apparent. Students noted the old wire fence that was falling down in spots, overgrown shrubbery, dead branches on the ground, loose and falling tombstones, and the lack of a sign identifying the cemetery. I was amazed that students thought a bench should be placed in the cemetery and flowers planted. They felt compelled to make improvements so we had more than enough service learning opportunities to tackle in the cemetery.

In June during the last week of school, a group of students volunteered to plant flowers at the cemetery after school. We had received a donation of flowers, and students were eager to dig up the ground and plant them in the spot where the historical maker would be placed in the fall. Without a nearby water source, we had to bring containers of water. One of the students and her mother volunteered to water the flowers throughout the summer as needed.

Not every cemetery is in such disrepair and needing attention. Nevertheless, possibilities for service learning exist. If a cemetery contains the graves of Civil

War veterans, special tombstones can be acquired for them. Other veterans may be eligible for recognition too. On special occasions, such as Flag Day or Memorial Day, small flags can be placed on graves of veterans. If that information is not known for those buried, flags can be placed randomly throughout the cemetery. Local veterans groups may assist the students and provide flags. Planting flowers and providing a bench might be appropriate, even for a cemetery in good condition. Interesting stories about various individuals buried in a cemetery inevitably exist and can be researched, written up, and then shared in local papers or presented to school and civic groups.

Student presentations to community groups as described previously are a form of service learning. Our team presentations were eye-opening experiences for our community's citizens, most of whom did not even know what a poor farm was or that one existed in our community. We informed them about how the poor farm had evolved into a hospital and then into a medical care facility. When our team did a presentation, students set up displays of the various activities from the project. Tombstone rubbings and data sheets giving the names of persons actually buried in the cemetery were popular items with an audience.

A small group of students would volunteer for such events if they occurred off school grounds or in the evening. A PowerPoint about the project was sometimes used, but most often it was the students themselves telling what they had done and showing materials developed. We shared our story with many groups from the school board to the county Historical Commission. In June our team hosted parents and other adults in a well-attended evening presentation with displays that were well received. The many educational presentations strengthened the school-community bonds markedly and brought the generations together in a very positive way.

Securing a historical marker

Securing a marker was appealing because the cemetery lacked a sign or any indication at all that it was an important part of local history. We followed through on what was needed to obtain a marker and learned a lot in the process. In early May, we returned to a Historical Commission meeting. Students presented the case for granting the cemetery a historical marker. They gave the commission a full and well-organized notebook containing the completed application, a list of people buried in the cemetery, historical documents from the team's research, an overview of the project and team activities, photographs taken during the project, and letters of support from our principal, the township supervisor, and from the students on the team.

In June, the president of the Historical Commission notified us that our application had been approved. The fee of $180 was paid out of the grant money to have a marker made—although we could have easily raised the money if grant funds were not available. The marker was completed in August and ready to be picked up. The marker itself was a fairly large metal plaque, so it was necessary to construct a small brick wall with an indentation for the marker. This was accomplished in the early fall. When the new school year began, the team of students that had procured the marker had, of course, moved up to 7th grade. Telling the new team members about the marker was a good introduction of the cemetery project to them. We ultimately decided to hold a marker dedication in early October when this year's team and last year's team could both attend.

On a beautiful Sunday afternoon in October, we dedicated the historical marker. Students had prepared invitations, which were sent to students from the previous year, parents, school officials, and other community members. Many students came with their families as did a number of citizens who read the recent article in the newspaper about the project that included an open invitation to the dedication. Several adults and students involved in the project spoke at the

Students were proud and had a real sense of satisfaction when the well-mounted historical marker drew praise from so many citizens.

ceremony. A reception was held after the ceremony in the community room of the nearby apartments, the site of the original poor farm building. Exhibits on all aspects of the project were displayed and students responded informally to questions as guests milled about and enjoyed the refreshments. It was especially gratifying to witness the now seventh graders confidently and effectively sharing what they had learned during the last school year.

The second year of the project provided a different service learning focus. Volunteers stayed after school to begin developing a plan for the booklet that would tell the story of the cemetery and our project. Over several weeks, students participated in various aspects of creating the booklet. We brainstormed what information would need to be in it. Students broke up into groups to work on the topics that had been generated. In most cases, students wrote a page or two on a topic and asked for examples of their work or historical documents to accompany what they had written. A cover and backing were added, and the school district printing office reproduced the 71-page booklet. Copies were distributed to local libraries, appropriate individuals and organizations, and students from the current and previous years. All the students took pride in having their work published and distributed in the community.

The service learning aspects of the project had a huge impact on students. They were excited about making a difference by participating in a real, meaningful activity. Indications of the impact this entire cemetery project had on students would appear from time to time. One parent told me that every time they would pass by the cemetery, her son would proclaim, "That's MY cemetery." Another instance occurred some years later when a former student chose for his Eagle Scout badge to clear away the rusty old wire fence in front of the cemetery and replace it with a magnificent, genuine split rail fence! I suspect, too, that when any of the students in the two teams attend a graveside service in the years ahead, they will recall "their" cemetery as they remember the highlight of their sixth grade education.

There are many resources available with ideas, examples, related resources, and lesson plans for conducting service learning projects. The National Service-Learning Clearinghouse has program examples, related research, and more (http://www.servicelearning.org). See also Learning In Deed (http://www. learningindeed.org). An excellent book is *The Complete Guide to Service Learning: Proven, Practical Ways to Engage Students in Civic Responsibility, Academic Curriculum & Social Action*. A revised second edition of this book written by Carolyn Berger Kaye was published in 2010 by Free Spirit Publishers. Another good resource to consult is *Service Learning in the Middle School: Building a Culture of Service* by Carl Fertman, George P. White, and Louis J. White (NMSA, 1996). It should be noted that many of the materials available continue to treat service learning as an independent entity, whereas in the middle school, service learning should be integrated with the curriculum and be an extension of the ongoing academic study.

CHAPTER

Reflections

Cemeteries: Alive with Learning has described many engaging and academically sound educational experiences that involved all the basic subject areas. These experiences were successful in part because they involved a cemetery, an unusual but rich setting for study. Because students often formed an attachment to the persons buried there, learning was more meaningful and lasting. The varied activities in this project contributed directly to fulfilling the thirteen major goals of middle level education (NMSA, 2010, pp. 11-12) and to meeting accepted state and national standards.

The educational effectiveness of this project was made evident in both informal and formal ways. The students completed an End of Year Cemetery Project Questionnaire that indicated the project was a very positive experience and noted those activities they valued the most. They felt they learned statistics well by using tombstone data to make charts and graphs and to do calculations. The graphing calculators were very popular and students were surprised by the graphs they could make. The after school small group field trips were definitely a favorite and several students mentioned with regret that they had been unable to attend one of them. Using microfilm and conducting research with the census and old newspapers made a big impression. Students really enjoyed hearing a research historian speak about the poor farm and life in our community around 1900. A number of students commented on how much they liked delivering presentations to in-school groups, the state representative, and various groups of adults. The students expressed their delight in the many hands-on activities and the opportunity for participating in learning experiences outside the classroom. It seems that every activity we did was especially valued by some segment of the team.

Benefits to students

Overall, students benefited in both small and large ways from their participation in this project. Academically, they improved in mastering the common skills of reading, writing, and speaking. Their reading improvement was due to the intense use of diverse sources of literature, from tombstone epitaphs to old newspapers to poetry. Improvement in writing involved equally diverse activities from evaluating a math graph to carefully describing an activity for a page in the cemetery booklet the team published and distributed. Most of the students improved their speaking skills well beyond what might normally be accomplished in a school year because they did so much of it. They were addressing real audiences about things they had learned and sharing the new knowledge they possessed.

Beyond growth in these basic areas, students had opportunities to advance their critical thinking skills in all academic subjects. We started with many mysterious and challenging questions in math and never stopped asking questions as we became involved with the other areas of the curriculum. In the process, students discovered the interrelationships of subjects and new resources like the census. They developed an awareness of and appreciation for the past through our studies. Due to the richness of the topics, differentiation was addressed as students could do further study in those areas that interested them the most. They were all learning how to learn.

In addition to these academic gains students benefited in other ways. The team bonded as we participated in this unusual educational adventure and the students got to know one another better. Other students, teachers, and staff in the school as well as parents and community members frequently asked about what we were currently doing in the cemetery project; our team soon gained a special identity as the team that was doing something "real." Students were proud to share our latest discoveries or what we were trying to figure out.

During the project, students also learned to build relationships with other adults that they encountered in our studies. They met many parents that helped at various times and attended our presentations. Students saw our gym teacher in a new light when she demonstrated one of her hobbies, paper cutting, (the expertise of J.B. Walker from the poor farm) and taught them the skill. Students also got to know well various community members, such as State Representative Whitmer and the research historian, Mrs. Davis, both of whom expressed admiration for what the team was doing. These experiences and others already noted went a long way to improving the self-concept of students. This was especially true for students who were not previously outgoing or noted as high achievers.

Benefits to parents

Parents benefited from this project too. Consistent communication through the team newsletters, the homework hotline, and more frequent conversations that students had at home kept parents informed about the project and encouraged their involvement. Many volunteered throughout the year by walking with us to the cemetery, driving students to after-school field trips, attending presentations on the project, and even watering flowers in the summer that we had planted at the cemetery. Parents frequently shared comments with me that their children made at home about the project, contributed ideas for additional activities, and thanked me for doing this project that had provided their children with new and valuable lessons that they would not normally have in school.

Benefits to teachers

Teachers gain immeasurably from designing and directing a cemetery-based study as well. Their sense of professional efficacy increases as students respond positively to the activities. In preparing for the project, I gained new skills when I took several technology classes during the summer and was able to use what I had learned during the school year. A class on Excel prepared me to set up a tombstone data spreadsheet and to produce the data in various formats—something I needed for the different graphs. Another professional development class showed me how to develop and maintain a website for the project. A week of graphing calculator classes enabled me to comfortably teach students how to make graphs from our tombstone data on the calculators. All the practice before and during the project with the computer programs, the digital camera, and the calculators made me a much more knowledgeable and confident teacher.

Designing the project was a challenge as I attempted to try something different that would motivate students and get them more involved in their education. I felt like we were on an adventure back in time. I was a fellow learner with students as we discovered discrepancies in the tombstone data and studied the poor farm history. I learned how to use the census materials and to work with microfilm as they did. Through the many activities we did, I became much better acquainted with my students as persons and as learners and was thus more able to guide their education.

For me, the cemetery project was an eye-opening experience. I came to realize that I was a creative teacher. Over the years, I had always changed my lesson plans and tried to improve them with hands-on motivating activities. I attended conferences, took classes, and read professional books in order to become a better teacher. But implementing the cemetery project took my teaching to another level. I had the good fortune to come across a grant that pushed me to come up with good ideas then organize them into a meaningful structure that brought together the important components of good middle school curriculum and instruction.

Benefits to school and community

The benefits of our cemetery project for others beyond our team far exceeded my expectations. The reputation of our entire school was enhanced as the team received publicity for the project and our local community gained knowledge about an important part of our community's history from our students. Both years newspapers carried stories of our activities to the general public. The Sunday afternoon dedication of the historical marker received favorable publicity in the newspaper and was filmed by the township television station for repeated showings the following week. A Detroit newspaper even carried a story about our project. When a group of students and I presented at a school board meeting, we appeared on the school district television station. Framed resolutions honoring our team came from the state legislature and the county board of commissioners.

The attention given our project did not stop with the local community or the state of Michigan. The Toyota TIME grant I received was a national grant administered by the National Council of Teachers of Mathematics (NCTM). A picture and brief story about the dedication of the historical marker were on the front page of the association's News Bulletin, an international publication. I presented the project at NCTM's annual conference in Philadelphia as well as at the state conference in Michigan. I also shared it with the other thirty-four Toyota TIME grant winners at a conference in Los Angeles. Since the project began, I have spoken to many groups ranging from educational associations to historical societies and will likely make additional presentations. I also had an article about the project published in *Teaching Tolerance* magazine. The students' tombstone data has been put on a website by a genealogical society. People from various regions of the country have contacted me on topics ranging from relatives being buried in the cemetery to questions on how to do a cemetery project. The project seems to have taken on a life of its own and it just keeps growing.

Beyond the cemetery

While I have shared many of the benefits of this project, there are some additional factors that should be considered. Perhaps no appropriate cemetery is available for use by students. Another everyday space such as a city park, a courthouse, or a baseball stadium could be the location for a holistic project that would give new meaning to your educational program. Any such place-based study can also be done by more than one team, sometimes an entire grade, or, in smaller schools, even the entire student body.

If a cemetery is available but one of the teachers in your team does not wish to participate or join in only on a minimal basis, the subject area for that teacher could be addressed in large group sessions, after school, or combined with another subject area. Perhaps your team schedule does not allow for large group time for sharing discoveries, doing presentations to guests, etc. Our team created such time when the daily schedule was rearranged for an assembly, standardized testing, or other special event. On some occasions we shortened academic classes ten minutes to get time needed. Obstacles can pop up in any project, but a little creative thinking can go a long way to solve, or at least minimize the problem. The benefits of a place-based project will outweigh the difficulties encountered.

Final thoughts

A special project like this does involve considerable work. Was it worth it? For me, it was the highlight of my teaching career. My experience from the cemetery project provided me with the skills and confidence to implement a new science-based project that involved the Red Cedar River and its watershed. I have now retired from teaching but I never tire of walking the dog to "my" cemetery to see the historical marker that we obtained or to tell someone in the community about the cemetery and poor farm that once existed there.

Postscript

I contacted the students who were on the teams during the first two years of the project and who are now in high school. I explained that I was writing a book for teachers about the cemetery project and included a release form that would permit me to use some of their work and pictures. Like the unfolding of the project itself, I was in for a surprise! The release forms were returned to me with numerous comments from students and parents. I was wished good luck with publishing and thanked many, many times over for doing the project. I received letters, notes, pictures, sticky notes, and comments written on the back of sealed envelopes – even a donation. I was truly overwhelmed with the responses indicating how meaningful the project was to students and families several years after they participated in it.

References

Dewhurst, C.K. & MacDowell, M. (1995). *Your wellwisher, J.B. Walker: A midwestern paper cut-out artist.* East Lansing, MI: Michigan State University.

Fertman, C., White, G., & White, L. (1996). *Service learning in the middle school: Building a culture of service.* Westerville, OH: National Middle School Association.

Kaye, Carolyn Berger. (2010). *The complete guide to service learning: Proven, practical ways to engage students in civic responsibility, academic curriculum, and social action.* Minneapolis, MN: Free Spirit Publishers.

Masters, Edgar Lee. (1915). *Spoon River anthology.* Retrieved January 14, 2009, from http://spoonriveranthology.net/spoon/river/originalOrder/

National Council for the Social Studies. (1994). *Expectations of excellence: Curriculum standards for social studies—Executive summary.* Retrieved January 2, 2009, from http://www.socialstudies.org/standards/execsummary

National Council of Teachers of English. (1998). NCTE/IRA standards for the English language arts. Retrieved December 31, 2008, from http://www.ncte.org/standards

National Council of Teachers of Mathematics. (2000). *Principles and standards for school mathematics.* Reston, VA: The National Council of Teachers of Mathematics, Inc.

National Middle School Association. (2010). *This we believe: Keys to educating young adolescents.* Westerville, OH.

National Science Teachers Association. (1996). *National science education standards.* Retrieved January 2, 2009, from http://www.nap.edu/openbook.php?record_id=4962&page=103

Toyota TIME grants available for innovative projects. (2003, December). News Bulletin ofNational Council of Teachers of Mathematics. 40, 1.

Vermont Old Cemetery Association. (1996). *Stones & bones: Using tombstones as textbooks.* Grafton,Vt: Author.

Appendix A
Related Resources

Association of Gravestone Studies. Retrieved March 18, 2010, from
www.gravestonestudies.org/publicaions.htm

This international association furthers the study and preservation of
gravestones. It publishes a journal, quarterly, newsletter, and special articles
in a FAQ format including a very helpful one, "Gravestone Rubbings:
Do's and Dont's."

Easley, L. M. (2005). Cemeteries as science labs. *Science Scope. 29*(3), 28-32.

This article gives cemetery activities focused on tombstone weathering.

Generation Networks, Inc. (2009). Ancestry.com. Retrieved May 15, 2009,
from http://www.ancestry.com

This site has many genealogy databases which require a paid subscription for
complete access. It is available in many libraries, including school libraries, at
no cost to the user.

Howells, Cyndi. (1996). *Cyndi's list.* Retrieved May 15, 2009, from
http://www.cyndislist.com/

This is a great starting point for a study of genealogical resources on
the Internet.

Lappan, G., Fey, J.T., Fitzgerald, W.M., Friel, S.N., & Phillips, E.D.
(1998). Data about us. In *Connected mathematics.* New York: Dale
Seymour Publications.

This booklet provided the order for the charts and graphs in the statistics unit.

Lowry, P. K. & McCrary, J.H. (2005). Science and history come alive in the
cemetery. *Science Scope. 29*(3), 33.

This article explains using the inquiry method for a student cemetery
walking tour.

McCabe, C. K. (2009). This teacher's tip: Visit the dead to wake your students. *neatoday. 27*(6), 39.

This article gives an overview of teacher Linda Prather's cemetery activities for 8th graders.

Prather, Linda. (1999, November). *Cemetery studies.* Retrieved May 10, 2009, from http://www.angelfire.com/ky2/cemetery/

This teacher's award-winning website provides lesson plans, student work, and an index to other websites that focus on cemetery studies.

Springer, M. (1994). *Watershed: A successful voyage into integrative learning.* Westerville, OH: National Middle School Association.

This book inspired me to use a theme to integrate academic subjects throughout a school year.

Woodward, E., Frost, S., & Smith, A. (1991, December). Cemetery mathematics. *Arithmetic teacher.* 31-36.

This article describes an eight day graphing unit using cemetery data.

Tombstone Data Chart

Ingham County Home Cemetery-Organizing Tombstone Data

Death Year		Total per decade	Death Year		Total per decade
1890	4		1910	6	
1891	6		1911	7	13
1892	4				
1893	6		1933	6	
1894	2		1934	5	
1895	2		1935	4	
1896	4		1936	3	
1897	7		1937	2	
1898	2		1938	3	
1899	5	42	1939	3	26
1900	5		1940	4	
1901	2		1941	2	6
1902	6		Unknown		6
1903	7				**142**
1904	9				
1905	4				
1906	3				
1907	4				
1908	4				
1909	5	49			

Appendix C
Graphing and Charting Tombstone Data Worksheet

1. Make a frequency table or chart in your notebook to organize the tombstone data by death years. See the sample below.

Chart for Tombstone Data

Death Year	Number of People
1890	4
1891	6
1892	4
and so on	
Unknown	

2. Put this data into a line plot. Group the data by decades. Use Xs for each person in that time period. See the sample below.

Line Plot for Tombstone Data

1890s	1900s	1910s	1920s	1930s	1940s

3. Make a bar graph on graph paper using this data. Group data by decades. *See the sample below.*

4. Please include titles and labels for your line plot and bar graph. How are they alike? How are they different? Find the mode/range in years.

Appendix D
Comparing Death Years and Death Ages with a Coordinate Graph

Use quarter inch grid paper to make a coordinate graph. Below the X axis, number each line starting with 1890, 1891, 1892… Label the X axis "Death Years".

Next to the Y axis, start with 0 and then number the lines 4, 8, 12, 16… Label the Y axis "Death Ages".

Use one of the tombstone data sheets to find the death year and age of death for each person. You must have both pieces of information to plot a point. Do not connect the points with lines. This type of a coordinate graph is a scatter plot.

If two people die the same year and have the same death age, put points next to each other at that spot.

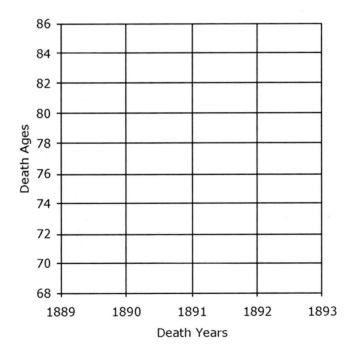

Tombstone Data Project

In this report you will collect the materials we have used in our study of the tombstone data for the cemetery and organize it as listed below. You will also write several paragraphs analyzing the graphs. Due date is _____.

Tombstone Data Analysis

Points

2 1. Report cover
   - Ingham County Home Cemetery Tombstone Data Analysis
   - Your name

2 2. Rubric (this paper)

2 3. Death Years data sheets

2 4. Death Age data sheets

2 5. Death Years chart

2 6. Line plot of death years

5 7. Paragraph analysis of the line plot
   - Explain what a line plot is and how it shows the tombstone data.
   - Find the mode and range for the death years and explain how you found it.

2 7. Bar graph of death years

5 8. Paragraph analysis of the bar graph
   - Explain what a bar graph is how it shows the tombstone data.
   - Which graph (line plot or bar graph) shows the death years data better? Why?
   - Are there any surprises or patterns in the data? Explain

2 9. Stem and leaf plot of death ages

5   10. Paragraph analysis of the stem and leaf plot
- Explain what a stem and leaf plot is and how it shows death age data.
- Find the range, mode, and median for the death ages and explain how you found it.
- When is the stem and leaf plot a good graph to use?

2   11. Back-to-back stem and leaf plot

5   12. Paragraph analysis of the back-to-back stem and leaf plot
- Explain what a stem and leaf plot is and how it shows death age data.
- Find the range, mode, and median for the death age of men and explain how you found it. Find the same information for women and explain how you found it.

2   13. Coordinate graph

5   14. Paragraph analysis of the coordinate graph
- Explain what a coordinate graph is and how it shows death years and death ages.
- When is a coordinate graph used for data?

5   15. Conclusion
- How might a historian use the data on these graphs to understand the Poor Farm in the late 1800s and early 1900s?

Appendix F
Percent in a Circle Graph (Decades) Worksheet

Fill in the chart using the given data.

Decades	Number of Deaths	Decimal	Percent	*Degrees
1890	42			
1900	49			
1910	13			
1920	0			
1930	26			
1940	6			
Unknown	6			
Total:	142			

* There are 360 degrees in a circle. To find the degrees for each group of years, multiply the decimal above times 360. Draw a circle on a blank sheet of paper. Place the ring of the angle ruler on the center and measure the degrees for each decade. Label the years and the percent of each section. Add color. Give the graph a title.

Percent in a Circle Graph (Death Ages) Worksheet

Fill in the chart below using data from the stem and leaf plot.

Death Ages in Years from Ingham County Home Cemetery

0	00
1	
2	7
3	25668
4	02368
5	0000111222458
6	0001123334556667899
7	00000001122233444555556666666788899
8	0012344556679
9	133348

Death Ages	Number of Deaths	Decimal	Percent	*Degrees
0–9				
10–19				
20–29				
30–39				
40–49				
50–59				
60–69				
70–79				
80–89				
90–99				
Unknown	44			
Total:	142			

* There are 360 degrees in a circle. To find the degrees for each group of years, multiply the decimal above times 360. Draw a circle on a blank sheet of paper. Place the ring of the angle ruler on the center and measure the degrees for each group of death years. Label the years and the percent of each section. Add color. Give the graph a title.

Appendix H
Cemetery Estimation Activity

Tree Circumference & Height

(You will need to do these activities with a partner.)

1. Walk up to one of the trees in the cemetery and put your hands around it.
   a. Do your hands touch?_____
   b. Estimate the distance around the tree in centimeters. _____cm (estimated circumference)
   c. Get a tape measure and measure the same distance around the tree. If the tree is too big, you may have to move the tape measure and use it more than once. _____cm (measured circumference)
   d. Compare your estimated circumference with the measured circumference. Did you make a good estimate? Explain. _____
   _____
   _____
   _____

2. One partner should stand next to your tree and the other person should move to the other side of the cemetery so you can see the whole tree.

   a. Estimate how many meters tall the tree is. _____ (Remember a meter is 3 feet and 3 inches long.)
   b. Now, estimate how many times taller the tree is than the partner standing next to it. _____
   c. Measure the height of the partner standing next to the tree by laying down on the sidewalk and measuring the partner's height using the tape measure. _____cm
   d. Multiply the answer in "b" times the answer in "c" to get the height of the tree. _____cm or _____meters (divide the cm by 100 because there are 100 cm in one meter.)
   e. Compare your answer in "a" with the answer in "d". Did you make a good estimate? Explain.
   _____
   _____
   _____

Appendix I
Cemetery Perimeter and Area

1. Go to the cemetery entrance and walk the length of the cemetery on the sidewalk.

   Estimate the length of the cemetery in meters. _____meters

2. Standing on the sidewalk at the entrance to the cemetery, walk to the back of the cemetery.

   Estimate the width of the cemetery. _____meters

3. Using your measurements in #3 and #4, find the perimeter of the cemetery in meters. _____ meters (2 lengths + 2 widths)

4. What is the length and width of the cemetery using the measuring wheel?

   _____length in meters   _____width in meters

   Find the perimeter of the cemetery using these numbers. _____meters

5. How do your estimates compare with the answers in #4? Explain.

   _____
   _____

6. What is the estimated area of the cemetery? _____ square meters (length times width)

Statistics Unit Survey

During our statistics unit we used some of the tombstone data for our graphs. We made a line plot and bar graph of death years, a stem and leaf plot of death ages, and a coordinate graph of death years and death ages. We did these graphs in place of practice problems from the math book.

1. Was our study of tombstone data and graphs helpful to you in learning about statistics? Please explain your answer.

2. Do you think the tombstone data and graphs were more interesting than practice problems from the book? Explain if possible.

3. Do you have any suggestions for other ways tombstone data and graphs could be used in the statistics unit?

4. We have used the graphing calculators to make tables of data and draw graphs. We will continue to use them during the school year. What do you like about the graphing calculators? Do you have any problems with the graphing calculators?

Over The Hill To The Poor House

---

by Will Carleton, 1897

Over the hill to the poor-house I'm trudgin' my weary way—
I, a woman of seventy, and only a trifle gray—
I, who am smart an' chipper, for all the years I've told,
As many another woman that's only half as old.
Over the hill to the poor-house—I can't quite make it clear!
Over the hill to the poor-house—it seems so horrid queer!
Many a step I've taken, a-toilin' to and fro,
But this is a sort of journey I never thought to go.

What is the use of heapin' on me a pauper's shame?
Am I lazy or crazy? am I blind or lame?
True, I am not so supple, nor yet so awful stout;
But charity ain't no favor, if one can live without.

I am ready and willin' an' anxious any day
To work for a decent livin' and pay my honest way;
For I can earn my victuals, an' more too, I'll be bound,
If anybody is willin' to only have me 'round.

Once I was young an' hand'some—I was, upon my soul—
Once my cheeks was roses, my eyes was black as coal;
And I can't remember, in them days, of hearin' people say,
For any kind of a reason, that I was in their way!

'Tain't no use of boastin' or talkin' over-free,
But many a house an' home was open then to me;
Many a han'some offer I had from likely men,
And nobody ever hinted that I was a burden then.

And when to John I was married, sure he was good and smart,
But he and all the neighbors would own I done my part;
For life was all before me, an' I was young an' strong,
And I worked my best an' smartest in tryin' to get along.

And so we worked together; and life was hard, but gay,
With now and then a baby to cheer us on our way.
Till we had half a dozen, an' all growed clean an' neat,
An' went to school like others, an' had enough to eat.

An' so we worked for the child'rn, and raised 'em every one—
Worked for 'em summer and winter, just as we ought to've done;
Only perhaps we humored 'em, which some good folks condemn,
But every couple's own child'rn's a heap the dearest to them!

Strange how much we think of OUR blessed little ones!—
I'd have died for my daughters, and I'd have died for my sons.
And God He made that rule of love; but when we're old and gray
I've noticed it sometimes, somehow, fails to work the other way.

Stranger another thing: when our boys an' girls was grown,
And when, exceptin' Charley, they'd left us there alone,
When John he nearer an' nearer came, an' dearer seemed to be,
The Lord of Hosts, He came one day an' took him away from me!

Still I was bound to struggle, an' never cringe or fall—
Still I worked for Charley, for Charley was now my all;
And Charley was pretty good to me, with scarce a word or frown,
Till at last he went a-courtin', and brought a wife from town.

She was somewhat dressy, an' hadn't a pleasant smile—
She was quite conceity, and carried a heap o' style;
But if ever I tried to be friends, I did with her, I know;
But she was hard and haughty, an' we couldn't make it go.

She had an edication, and that was good for her,
But when she twitted me on mine, 'twas carryin' things too far,
An' I told her once, 'fore company, (an' it almost made her sick)
That I never swallowed a grammer, nor 'et a 'rithmetic.

So 'twas only a few days before the thing was done—
They was a family of themselves, and I another one.
And a very little cottage one family will do,
But I never have seen a mansion that was big enough for two.

An' I never could speak to suit her, never could please her eye,
An' it made me independent, an' then I didn't try.
But I was terribly humbled, an' felt it like a blow,
When Charley turned agin me, an' told me I could go!

I went to live with Susan, but Susan's house was small,
And she was always a-hintin' how snug it was for us all;
And what with her husband's sisters, and what with child'rn three,
'Twas easy to discover there wasn't room for me.

An' then I went with Thomas, the oldest son I've got:
For Thomas's buildings'd cover the half of an acre lot,
But all the child'rn was on me—I couldn't stand their sauce—
And Thomas said I needn't think I was comin' there to boss.

An' then I wrote to Rebecca, my girl who lives out West,
And to Isaac, not far from her—some twenty miles at best;
And one of 'em said 'twas too warm there for anyone so old,
And t'other had an opinion the climate was too cold.

So they have shirked and slighted me, an' shifted me about—
So they have well nigh soured me, an' wore my old heart out;
But still I've borne up pretty well, an' wasn't much put down,
Till Charley went to the poor-master, an' put me on the town!

Over the hill to the poor-house—my child'rn dear, good-bye!
Many a night I've watched you when only God was nigh;
And God'll judge between us; but I will al'ays pray
That you shall never suffer the half that I do to-day!

Appendix L
Tombstone Geology Activity

Purpose: To identify tombstone rock and to examine the weathering of it.

Safety and Courtesy Rules:
1. Do not climb or sit on tombstones.
2. Respect cemetery property.

Cemetery Map: Draw a map of the cemetery using the Cemetery Map Rubric as your guide. Include Dobie Road, fences, trees in the cemetery, tombstones, and the historical marker.

Chart Directions: Select 7 tombstones and fill in the Tombstone Chart. You should have 3 different rock types.

Part A Write the name on the tombstone.

Part B Write the birth date.

Part C Write the date of death.

Part D Compute and record the number of years since the tombstone was placed. (Current year minus year of death.)

Part E Identify the rock type. Use the rock key below and teacher samples.

Part F Use the weathering key to identify the degree of weathering. Write the number from the weathering key in this column.

Part G Number the tombstone location on your map.

Part H Describe any special conditions that might have affected the weathering of the tombstone.

Rock Key

1. *Limestone*—usually gray, white, or tan. Does not take a high polish. Feels rough. (sedimentary)

2. *Sandstone*—light colored i.e. white, buff, pink, brown, reddish, yellow-orange. Feels sandy to the touch. Looks as it is made of sand grains. Usually not polished. (sedimentary)

3. *Slate*—black, brown, red or dark grey. Looks like a clean blackboard. (metamorphic)

4. *Marble*—colors of limestone, sometimes pink or greenish or black. Highly polished. Recrystallized. (metamorphic)

5. *Granite* – light colored, pink or grey. Made of made of large crystals. Highly polished. (igneous)

6. *Gneiss* – made of crystals. Minerals can be arranged in thick parallel bands. Minerals are quartz, feldspar, and mica. (metamorphic)

7. *Cement* – white or gray. A mixture of very small stones.

Weathering Key

1 – unweathered, corners sharp, stone looks new

2 – weathered surface is rough, letters worn but can be read

3 – heavily weathered, some letters or numbers missing or too faded to see

Questions:

1. What seemed to be the most common tombstone rock in this cemetery?

2. Which tombstone rock seemed to be the most durable?

3. What factors might influence the choice of rock for a tombstone?

Appendix M
Tombstone Chart for Geology Activity

Tombstone	1	2	3	4	5	6	7
Name							
Birth date							
Death date							
Marker age							
Rock type							
Weathering							
Location							
Notes							

Cemetery Map Rubric

You will make a rough draft map of the cemetery on the back of this paper. Tomorrow in class you will have time to draw a final draft. Your final draft should have the following:

_____ rows of tombstones   5

_____ large trees inside cemetery   2

_____ fence around parts of the cemetery   2

_____ opening into the cemetery   2

_____ Dobie Road (label on map)   2

_____ sidewalk   2

                                 _____**15 points**

Your final draft should also include the following:

_____ compass rose   3

_____ key with symbols   3

_____ use of color   3

_____ neatness   3

_____ name of cemetery given as a title –
Ingham County Home Cemetery   1

_____ your name on the back   1

_____ this rubric attached   1

                                 _____**15 points**

                                 _____**30 points total**

Appendix O
The Ingham County Home Cemetery

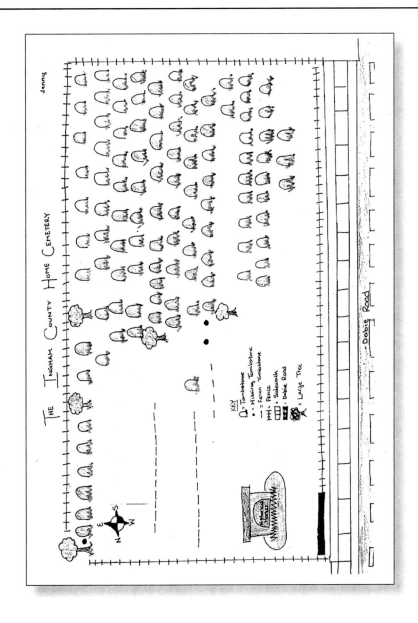

LaVergne, TN USA
26 April 2010
180474LV00001B/3/P

9 781560 902386